THE WATER'S EDGE
In Cross Stitch

THE WATER'S EDGE
In Cross Stitch

Jayne Netley Mayhew
and Nicki Wheeler

David & Charles

To Ian, for every stitch that you felt
To Tim, for every word that you heard
Thanks for all your love and support

For our Boris and Nelke

*Page 2: A fun collection of sea creatures including a rug, stuffed toys and
baby bricks (see page 111)*

First published in the UK in 1999
Reprinted 1999
Designs, charts and illustrations Copyright © Jayne Netley Mayhew 1999
Text Copyright © Jayne Netley Mayhew and Nicki Wheeler 1999
Photography and layout Copyright © David & Charles 1999

ISBN 0 7153 0703 7

Photography by Di Lewis
Book design by Carol McCleeve
Printed in Great Britain by Butler & Tanner Ltd
for David & Charles
Brunel House   Newton Abbot   Devon

CONTENTS

INTRODUCTION

The theme of this, our third book, is the water's edge, in which we follow the journey of water from rivers, ponds and lakes, to the estuary and out to sea, finally ending at the polar regions. As with our other books, *Animals in Cross Stitch* and *Four Seasons in Cross Stitch*, we have included a mixture of native and exotic wildlife and flowers. The varied wildlife includes birds, fishes, insects, reptiles, mammals and beautiful wild flowers that can be found in and around the water. The designs also include other watery motifs – boats, anchors, buckets, spades and shells. The book is split into three sections, Ponds and Lakes, Rivers and Estuaries and All at Sea, each depicting the various flowers and wildlife to be found in these habitats. Each section's projects are illustrated by beautiful colour photographs, with full instructions for stitching and making up the items shown. A mixture of stranded cotton (floss), metallic threads, tapestry wool (yarn) and beads are used to work the projects using a variety of stitches, including cross stitch, three-quarter cross stitch, half cross stitch, French knots and backstitch.

The projects for Ponds and Lakes include frogs basking in the summer sun on top of lily pads, colourful dragonflies, humorous hippos, delicate pink flamingos and wild flowers. The designs for the Rivers and Estuaries section show magnificent white Camargue horses galloping through swamplands, elegant swans, bright kingfishers, leaping salmon and brown bears feasting on fish at the river's edge. The projects in All at Sea include a stunning rock-pool collage of brightly coloured fish and shells, a beautiful clipper ship in full sail on the high seas, playful dolphins and a polar bear and cub playing in the snow.

We have included designs which are suitable for stitchers of all abilities. For the beginner there are small sea creatures, dragonflies, humorous hippo desk accessories and a variety of pretty wild flowers, providing no end of inspiration for gifts and ideas. Some designs such as the clipper ship fire-screen and rock-pool collage may look complicated but are worked in whole cross stitches using tapestry wool (yarn). The colours for stranded cotton (floss) are also listed on the keys so that you can stitch them up in silk threads if you wish. For the more experienced stitcher, a selection of large projects such as the Camargue horses, playful dolphins and cormorant would prove to be an enjoyable challenge. Some designs are complemented by the addition of metallic threads and beads to give extra sparkle and texture to the completed embroideries. Some of the designs included in this book are available as mail order kit packs by Janlynn. Further details of materials used can be found in Stockists on page 127. We hope that you will have as much pleasure from using this book as we have had working on it. Happy stitching.

Jayne Netley Mayhew and Nicki Wheeler

Left: *The Emperor Penguins Picture (see page 122) and the Sea Creatures Cushion and Baby Bricks (see page 111) are just three ways in which the authors bring the theme of the water's edge to life*

GETTING STARTED

One of the reasons why cross stitch is so popular, apart from being so easy to work, is that the designs are simple to adapt: merely by changing the materials used – the fabric, the thickness or type of thread or the background colour – a design can be transformed, and examples of this are given throughout the book.

MATERIALS

FABRICS

Most of the designs in this book have been worked on Aida fabric with 14 blocks or threads to one inch (2.5cm), often called 14-count Aida. Some designs use a larger or smaller count Aida or an evenweave fabric such as linen. The same design stitched on fabrics of different counts will work up as different sizes. The larger the count (eg 18-count), the more threads per inch (2.5cm), therefore the smaller the design. The smaller the count (eg 6-count), the fewer threads per inch (2.5cm), therefore the larger the design.

Some of the designs are worked on very fine fabrics such as the Waterside Flowers table linen. These designs can be hard work on the eyes, so you could use half cross stitch, or a slightly larger count Aida or evenweave fabric, which would make the design larger. Each project lists the type of fabric used, giving the thread count and fabric name, which should be quoted when purchasing goods. All DMC threads and fabrics can be purchased from good needlework shops. The finished size of each design is also given, but you can experiment by using different fabric counts to achieve surprising effects. Before starting a piece of work, always check the thread and stitch count to ensure that the design will fit the intended frame.

THREADS

If you want your designs to look exactly the same as those shown in the photographs, use the colours and threads listed for each project. The threads used in this book are DMC stranded cotton (floss), tapestry wool (yarn) and metallic threads.

Stranded cotton (floss) This is the most widely used embroidery thread and is available in hundreds of colour shades, including silver and gold metallic. It is a lustrous, mercerised thread, which has a smooth finish and a slight sheen. It is made from six strands twisted together to form a thick thread, which can be used whole or split into thinner strands. The type of fabric used will determine how many strands of thread you will need to use: most of the designs in this book use two strands of thread for cross stitch and one strand for backstitch.

Tapestry wool (yarn) DMC wool is a matt, hairy yarn made from 100% wool. It is made from short fibres twisted together to make a thick single thread which cannot be split. Designs using tapestry wool are usually worked on canvas using one or two strands. A wide selection of colours is available, with shades tending to be slightly duller than for stranded cotton (floss).

Metallic threads These vary quite considerably in texture and fibre content. Some are thick, single threads made from a mixture of viscose, nylon and metallised polyester, whilst finer threads are often made from metallised polyester or Lurex and have a flat appearance.

Thread management Always keep threads tidy and manageable. Thread organisers and project cards are ideal for this purpose. Cut the threads to equal lengths and loop them into project cards with the thread shade code and colour key symbol written at the side. This will prevent threads from becoming tangled and the shade codes being lost.

EQUIPMENT

Needles Stitch your designs using a tapestry needle which has a large eye and blunt end to prevent damage to the fabric. Choose a size of needle which will slide easily through the holes of the fabric without distorting or enlarging them. You will problably find it easier to sew if you use a thimble, especially for projects that use canvas.

Scissors You will need a sharp pair of embroidery scissors for cutting threads and a pair of dressmaking scissors for cutting fabric.

Frames Your work will be easier to handle and stitches will be kept flat and smooth if you mount your fabric on to an embroidery hoop or frame which will accommodate the whole design. Bind the outer ring of an embroidery hoop with white bias tape to prevent it from marking the fabric. This will also keep the fabric taut and prevent it from slipping whilst you are working.

TECHNIQUES

The following techniques and tips will help you attain a professional finish by showing you how to prepare for work and care for your finished embroidery.

Each project gives the finished size of a design when worked on the recommended fabric, together with the amount of fabric needed. The fabric size is at least 8–10cm (3–4in) larger than the finished size of the design to allow for turnings or seam allowances when mounting the work or making it up into gifts. Measurements are given in metric with the imperial equivalent in brackets. Always use either metric or imperial – do not try to mix the two.

When making up any item, a 1.5cm (⅝in) seam allowance has been used unless otherwise stated. Instructions for making up are included under each project, where appropriate. If making up a garment such as a waistcoat, mark out the pattern pieces on to the fabric before you start stitching to ensure each design is correctly placed. To prevent fabric from fraying, machine stitch around the edges or bind with tape.

To find the centre point from which to start stitching, tack (baste) a row of stitches horizontally and vertically from the centre of each side of the fabric – these correspond to the arrows at the sides of each chart.

Each project in this book includes a colour photograph of the worked design, a colour chart and key, instructions for stitching and making up the designs as gifts and accessories, and occasionally graphs and other diagrams.

USING THE CHARTS AND KEYS

All the designs in this book use DMC embroidery fabrics, stranded cotton (floss) or tapestry yarn (wool). The colours and symbols shown on the colour key correspond to DMC shade codes. Each project lists the number of skeins required for each thread colour together with a colour name, which is given for easy reference only – when purchasing threads, use the correct shade code numbers. Each chart is in full colour, using colours that match the thread shades as closely as possible. Each coloured square on the chart represents one complete cross stitch and some squares also have a symbol in them. The colours and symbols correspond to those listed in the key at the side of each chart. The number at the side of each box corresponds to the DMC shade code.

A quarter square represents a three-quarter cross stitch. French knots or beads are indicated by a coloured square, usually with a circle or sometimes a small symbol at the centre – the project instructions specify which to use. If you wish to use stranded cotton (floss) to work cross stitches or French knots rather than beads, the code numbers for both are given. In some cases a French knot is represented by a small white spot for the eye highlights, such as the Polar Bears Picture. The solid coloured line indicates backstitch. Small black arrows at the sides of a chart indicate the centre, and by lining these up you will find the centre point. Some of the larger charts are spread over four pages with the colour key repeated on each double page. To prevent mistakes, work systematically so that you read the chart accurately. Constantly check your progress against the chart and count the stitches as you go. If your sight is poor you may find it helpful to enlarge a chart on a colour photocopier.

USING THE GRAPHS

Graphs are used to indicate where to place designs on the fabric, for example in the Sea Creatures Rug on page 111. Graphs are also used to produce templates for making gifts and accessories, as in the Frog and Lilies Tea Cosy (see fig 13, page 17). Each square on the graph represents 5cm (2in). Transfer the template on to ready-printed dressmakers' paper, or draw your own graph paper. The templates have either a 6mm (¼in) or 1.5cm (⅝in) seam allowance included – this is indicated in the project instructions.

MAKING BIAS BINDING

1. To make bias strips, fold over a corner of fabric at a 45° angle, then cut along the diagonal fold to give a bias edge. Use a pencil and ruler to mark out the diagonal lines on the fabric 5cm (2in) apart, then cut along the pencilled lines to make the bias strips (fig 1).
2. With right sides facing, place the bias strips at right angles so that the short diagonal edges meet. Stitch along these edges, then press the seam open. Repeat this process until your strip reaches the required length (fig 2).
3. To make the binding, press a 1cm (½in) turning to the wrong side along each long edge, then bring the folds together, enclosing the raw edges and press. The binding is now ready.

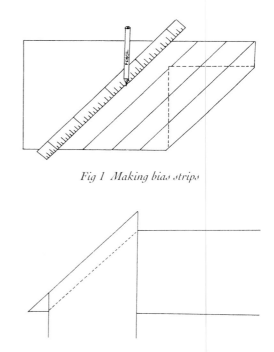

Fig 1 Making bias strips

Fig 2 Sewing bias strips together

WASHING AND PRESSING FINISHED WORK

If your work has become grubby during stitching, gently hand wash in warm water using a mild liquid detergent. Use a soft nail brush to remove any stubborn marks, rinse in clean water, place the damp fabric on a clean white towel and leave to dry on a flat surface. Do not iron directly on to your work as this will flatten the stitches and spoil the finished effect. Lay the work face down on a clean, white towel, cover with a clean, fine cloth and then press.

MOUNTING AND FRAMING

Take larger pictures to a professional framer, who will be able to stretch the fabric correctly and cut any surrounding mounts accurately. If mounting work into fire-screens or footstools, follow the manufacturer's instructions. For smaller pieces, back with lightweight iron-on interfacing to prevent the fabric wrinkling, and then mount into plastic flexi-hoops, trinket boxes, coasters, cards etc, following the manufacturer's instructions.

STITCH GUIDE

Cross stitch embroidery is a simple and straight-forward technique. The designs may look complicated but the effects are achieved by the clever use of colour and stitch work. In this book, detail is added by the use of three-quarter cross stitch, half cross stitch, backstitch and French knots, with the addition of beads and metallic threads.

The following diagrams show you how to work all the stitches used. When following the stitch instructions, please note that one block or thread refers to one block of Aida fabric or one thread of evenweave fabric.

STARTING AND FINISHING THREAD

To start off your first length of thread, make a knot at one end and push the needle through to the back of the fabric, about 3cm (1¼in) from your starting point, leaving the knot on the right side. Stitch towards the knot, securing the thread at the back of the fabric as you go (fig 3). When the thread is secure, cut off the knot.

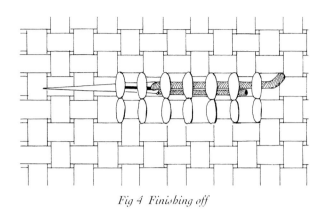

Fig 4 Finishing off

CROSS STITCH

Each coloured square on the chart represents one complete cross stitch. Cross stitch is worked in two easy stages. Start by working one diagonal stitch over one block or thread, then work a second diagonal stitch over the first stitch, but in the opposite direction to form a cross (fig 5). The Wild Duck Draught Excluder and the sea shell border of the Rock-pool Shells Throw have been worked over two blocks or threads to give a larger stitch (fig 6).

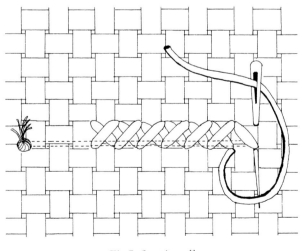

Fig 3 Starting off

To finish off a thread or start new threads, simply weave the thread into the back of several worked stitches (fig 4).

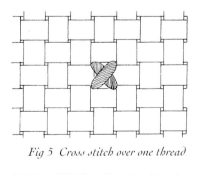

Fig 5 Cross stitch over one thread

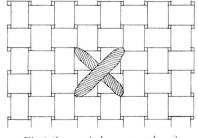

Fig 6 Cross stitch over two threads

If you have a large area to cover, work a row of half cross stitches in one direction and then work back in the opposite direction with diagonal stitches to complete each cross. The upper stitches of all the crosses should lie in the same direction to produce a neat effect (fig 7).

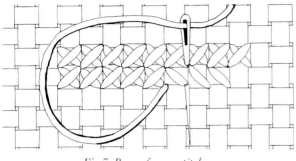

Fig 7 Rows of cross stitches

THREE-QUARTER CROSS STITCH

A small coloured square taking up a quarter of a square on the chart represents a three-quarter cross stitch. Forming three-quarter cross stitches on Aida is less accurate than on evenweave or linen fabric because the centre of the square block needs to be pierced.

Work the first half of a cross stitch in the normal way, then work the second diagonal stitch from the opposite corner but insert the needle at the centre of the cross, forming three-quarters of the complete stitch. A square showing two smaller coloured squares in opposite corners indicates that two of these stitches will have to be made back to back (fig 8).

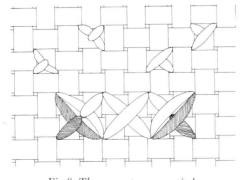

Fig 8 Three-quarter cross stitch

HALF CROSS STITCH

This stitch is used for the Clipper Ship Firescreen, page 102, which is worked in tapestry wool (yarn). A half cross stitch is simply one half of a cross stitch, with the diagonal facing the same way as the upper stitches of each complete cross stitch (fig 9).

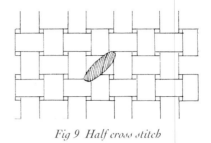

Fig 9 Half cross stitch

BACKSTITCH

Backstitch is indicated on charts by a solid coloured line. It is worked around areas of completed cross stitches to add definition, or on top of stitches to add detail.

To work backstitch, start by pulling the needle through the hole in the fabric at 1 (fig 10), then push back through at 2. For the next stitch, pull the needle through at 3, push to the back at 1, then repeat the process to make the next stitch. This will give you short stitches at the front of your work and a longer stitch at the back. If working backstitch over two blocks or threads, such as when using Abbey (Afghan) evenweave fabric, work each stitch over two threads.

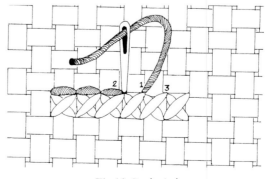

Fig 10 Backstitch

FRENCH KNOTS

These are small knots which are used to add detail, for example, as the eye highlights on the Polar Bears Picture. They are indicated on the chart by a small white spot. Some designs, such as the Waterside Flowers table linen, use large areas of French knots and in this case they are indicated by a coloured square usually with a circle or sometimes a small symbol at the centre.

To work this stitch, bring the needle through to the front of the fabric and wind the thread tightly once around the needle. Hold the twisted thread firmly in place and carefully insert the needle one thread away from its starting position (fig 11). For a larger knot, twist the thread two or three times around the needle.

ADDING BEADS

Beads are indicated on the charts by a coloured square with a circle at the centre. With the needle at the right side of the fabric, thread the bead over the needle and on to the thread, then attach it to the fabric by working the first half of a cross stitch (fig 12). All stitches must run in the same direction so that the beads lie in neat rows on the fabric.

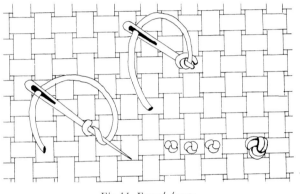

Fig 11 French knots

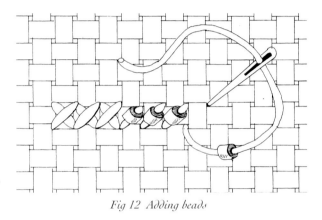

Fig 12 Adding beads

TECHNIQUE TIPS

• Steam press your embroidery fabric before stitching to remove any stubborn creases.

• Mount fabric onto an embroidery frame or hoop to keep stitches smooth and flat.

• Work cross stitches with the top threads all facing in the same direction.

• Thread up lengths of several colours of stranded cotton (floss) into needles, and then arrange these at the side of your work by shade code number or by key reference.

• Work the designs from the centre outwards, or split them into workable sections such as quarters. On larger designs, first work the main subject and then complete the background.

• When taking threads across the back of a design, weave the thread through the back of existing stitches to avoid any ugly lines showing on the right side.

• Use short lengths of thread – about 30cm (12in) – to reduce any knotting and tangling.

• Check your work constantly against the chart to avoid making mistakes.

• For a smooth piece of work without any lumps or bumps, avoid using knots at the back of your work, and cut off any excess threads as short as possible.

• Keep your work clean by packing it away in its own clean plastic bag to prevent any accidents.

Ponds & Lakes

This collection of designs represents the wonderful abundance of common and exotic wildlife to be found in and around our ponds and lakes.

After the cold winter, spring sun warms the water and creatures begin to stir among the weeds and mud at the bottom of ponds and lakes. Frogs and fish lay their eggs and very soon the waters are bursting with new life. In the summer, pond creatures such as tadpoles, dragonflies, fish and birds feed greedily to fatten themselves up, to prepare for the colder, leaner days to follow.

Celebrate this abundance of wildlife with our lazy frog and water-lilies design, worked on white and yellow 14-count Aida, combined with pretty gingham fabric to make colourful kitchen accessories. There is also a picture of a superb and realistic golden common carp and a dragonflies and irises waistcoat and bell pull, worked on 14-count Aida and 28-count linen respectively.

During midsummer, ponds are fringed with colourful blooms, like purple loosestrife, fragrant water-mint, meadowsweet and grasses. These have been used to work pretty table linen. Flowers and foliage also provide food, shelter and nesting sites for pond life and water fowl, and we have worked a selection of colourful ducks in a row to make a picture and an unusual draught excluder. If you prefer more exotic creatures, why not have a go at working the wallowing happy hippos to make fun office accessories, or the pretty pink flamingos picture, showing these gorgeous birds feeding in the soda lakes.

Frog and Lilies

The delightful tea cosy, tray and place-mats pictured on page 14 have been decorated with a lovely little frog, lazing on the lily pads on a bright sunny day. A variety of cross stitch, three-quarter cross stitch, backstitch and a tiny French knot are used to work the frog and white water-lilies, which are bordered by wispy grasses and delicate flowers. The colours of the design are complemented by the use of white, buff and yellow Aida.

Frog and Lilies Tea Cosy

FINISHED DESIGN SIZE
20.5cm (8in) square approximately

WHAT YOU WILL NEED
- Lemon 14-count Aida, 50 x 56cm (19¾ x 22in)
- Cotton backing fabric, 50 x 56cm (19¾ x 22in)
- Medium-weight polyester wadding (batting), 50 x 90cm (⅝yd x 36in) wide
- Lining fabric, 50 x 90cm (⅝yd x 36in) wide
- Contrast bias binding, 1.6m (1¾yd)
- Matching sewing thread
- Paper for template

DMC STRANDED COTTON (FLOSS)
1 SKEIN
Black 310; white; very dark parrot green 904; dark parrot green 905; med parrot green 906; light parrot green 907; copper 921; light copper 922; very pale yellow 3823; light pine green 772; light yellow green 3348; med yellow green 3347; topaz 725; very light topaz 727; very light brown grey 3024; med grey brown 3022; very dark coffee brown 938; dark coffee brown 801; med brown 433; dark golden brown 975; golden brown 3826; med golden brown 976; light golden brown 977; very light golden brown 3827; very light old gold 677; med antique blue 931; light antique blue 932

1. Prepare your fabric for work, reading the Techniques section if necessary. Refer to the Stitch Guide pages 11–13 for how to work the stitches, working the design from the centre outwards. Work the frog and lilies first, then fill in the background water and grasses.

2. When stitching the design use two strands of stranded cotton (floss) for the cross stitch and three-quarter stitch.

3. Work the backstitch detail using two strands of stranded cotton (floss) in dark parrot green 905 for the yellow flower stems. Use one strand of very dark coffee brown 938 to outline the frog's body, black 310 for the eye, med yellow green 3347 for the grass stems, med brown 433 for the white flower stems and med brown grey 3022 to work around each lily petal. Work a French knot, using one strand of white, for the small highlight on the frog's eye.

TO MAKE UP THE TEA COSY

1. Draw a template of the tea cosy pattern (fig 13), see Using Graphs page 10 for instructions. Place the template over the stitched design and cut one shape in Aida and one in backing fabric. Then cut two shapes each from wadding (batting) and lining fabric.

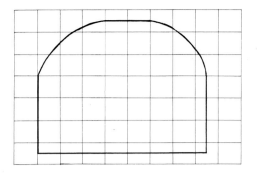

Fig 15 Tea cosy template

2. With right sides down, lay the lining shapes side by side on a flat surface. Place one wadding (batting) shape on top of each lining shape. Then, with right sides up, place the embroidered Aida and the cotton backing fabric shapes, one on top of each wadding shape, sandwiching the wadding between the two fabric layers. Tack (baste) fabric and wadding together to form the front and back pieces of the tea cosy.

3. Bind the bottom straight edge of each tea cosy shape with a ready-made decorative bias binding or make your own (see Making Bias Binding page 10).

4. To attach the binding, open out the folded edges, lay the binding along the edge to be bound so that right sides are facing and all the raw edges match. Pin, tack (baste) and stitch along the fold line, taking a 1cm (½in) seam allowance. Turn the binding down and over to the wrong side, to form an edging. Fold in the raw edge of the binding so that it covers the line of machine stitches, and hand stitch in place along the folded edge (fig 14).

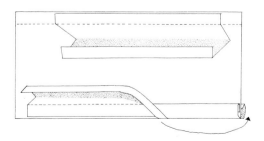

Fig 14 Attaching bias binding

5. With right sides out, and linings facing, place the front and back tea cosy shapes together. Pin, tack (baste) and machine stitch round the curved edge, taking a 1cm (½in) seam allowance. To finish, bind the curved edge of the tea cosy with decorative bias binding.

Frog and Lilies Place-Mats

FINISHED DESIGN SIZE
10 x 20.5cm (4 x 8in) approximately

WHAT YOU WILL NEED FOR EACH PLACE-MAT
- White 14-count Aida, 23 x 33cm (9 x 13in)
- Contrast cotton fabric, 30 x 90cm (⅜yd x 36in) wide
- Medium-weight polyester wadding (batting), 28 x 42cm (11 x 16½in)
- Contrast bias binding, 1.6m (1¾yd)
- Matching sewing thread
- Ricrac braid, 90cm (1yd)

DMC STRANDED COTTON (FLOSS)
Use the thread list for the Frog and Lilies Tea Cosy omitting med yellow green 3347

1. Follow step 1 on page 16 for the tea cosy, using the same chart but only working the frog, water-lilies and water in the foreground, omitting the background foliage, water-lilies and water.

2. When stitching the design use two strands of stranded cotton (floss) for the cross stitch and one strand for the backstitch and French knots.

3. Work the backstitch detail using dark coffee brown 938 to outline the frog's body, black 310 for the eye, and med brown grey 3022 around each lily petal. Work a French knot in white for the small highlight on the frog's eye.

TO MAKE UP EACH PLACE-MAT
1. For each place-mat, cut two 28 x 42cm (11 x 16½in) rectangles from cotton fabric and one from wadding (batting). Trim away excess Aida fabric from the completed design, to leave a 15 x 26cm (6 x 10¼in) patch.

Above: *A water-lily detail from the main chart provides a pretty motif for a napkin*

DMC

▦	932	▦	725
▦	931	▦	3347
▨	677	# #	3348
4 4 / 4 4	3827	▦	772
▦	977	O O	3823
↑ ↑	976	Z Z / Z Z	922
▦	3826	▦	921
▦	975	▦	907
▦	433	▌▌	906
▦	801	▦	905
▦	938	▌▌	904
▦	3022	~ ~	white
▨	3024	■	310
2 2 / 2 2	727		

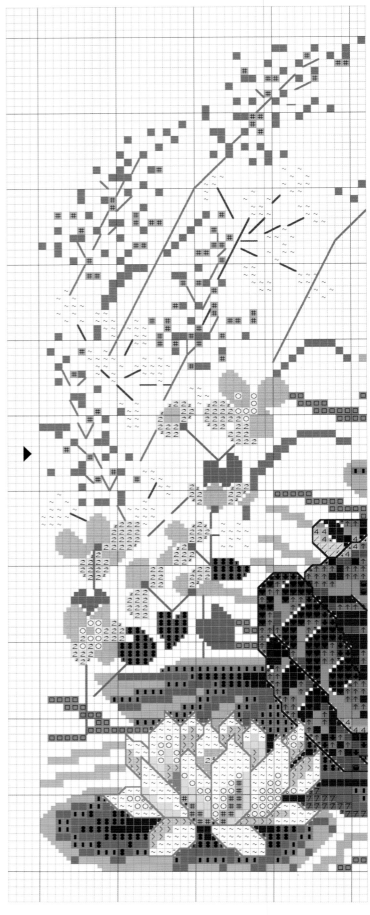

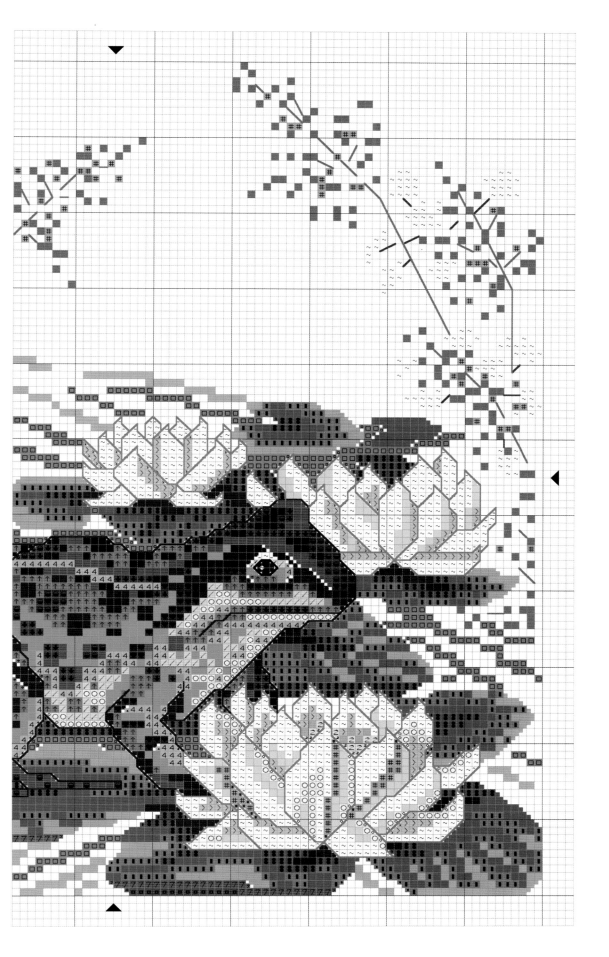

2. For the place-mat front, pin and tack (baste) the embroidered patch centrally to the right side of one cotton rectangle. Machine stitch the patch in place, making a row of stitches 1cm (½in) from the outer edges, then stitch ricrac braid neatly over the machine stitches to make a border. To finish the patch, create a frayed edging by teasing out the threads at the outer edges.

3. Lay the remaining cotton shape right side down on a flat surface. Place the wadding (batting) shape on top, then lay the place-mat front, with right side up, on top, so that the wadding is sandwiched between the two fabric layers. Pin and tack (baste) the fabric and wadding layers together.

4. To finish, bind around the straight edges of the place-mat with a ready-made decorative bias binding or make your own. Refer to Making Bias Binding page 10 for instructions. To attach the binding, follow step 4 on page 17 of the making up instructions as for the Frog and Lilies Tea Cosy.

Frog and Lilies Napkins

FINISHED DESIGN SIZE
3.5 x 5cm (1½ x 2in) approximately

WHAT YOU WILL NEED FOR EACH NAPKIN
• Christmas green 27-count Linda (E1235), or other linen or evenweave fabric, 33cm (13in) square
• Matching sewing thread

DMC STRANDED COTTON (FLOSS)
1 SKEIN
White; very pale yellow 3823; light pine green 772; light yellow green 3348; topaz 725; very light topaz 727; very light brown grey 3024; med grey brown 3022

1. Prepare your fabric for work, reading the Techniques section if necessary. Neaten the raw edges of each napkin by pressing up a 1cm (½in) turning, then stitch the hem in place.

Hand embroider to make a decorative hem if you wish. This hemming could be done after the embroidery if you prefer. Refer to the Stitch Guide pages 11–13 to work the stitches.

2. Work the small lily design (the lily in the left-hand corner of the chart on page 18) at the bottom right-hand corner of each napkin. Use two strands of stranded cotton (floss) for the cross stitch and one strand for the backstitch, worked over two threads of evenweave fabric.

3. Work the backstitch in med brown grey 3022 around each lily petal.

Frog and Lilies Tray

FINISHED DESIGN SIZE
20.5cm (8in) square approximately

WHAT YOU WILL NEED
• Parchment 14-count Aida, 56cm (22in) square
• Tray for embroidery (available from Framecraft – see Stockists page 127)

DMC STRANDED COTTON (FLOSS)
Use the thread list for the Frog and Lilies Tea Cosy on page 16

1. Follow steps 1–3 on page 16 for the frog and lilies tea cosy, using the same chart.

2. To complete your tray, follow the manufacturer's instructions.

FROGS
Frogs spend much of their time, especially the summer months, on land and return to the water in the early spring to mate and spawn. The tiny tadpoles swim around in clumps, because they are vulnerable to predators like fish, newts and insects. As they become bigger, the tadpoles learn to hide but only a lucky few survive to grow into frogs.

Wild Ducks

This charming collection of wild ducks – from left to right, the pochard, teal, wigeon, tufted duck and goldeneye – can be seen during the winter months in freshwater ponds and lakes. This versatile design can be worked as a picture on 14-count Aida or as a draught excluder using a larger stitch. Both projects use a mixture of cross stitch, three-quarter cross stitch and backstitch.

Wild Duck Picture

FINISHED DESIGN SIZE
16 x 47cm (6¼ x 18½in) approximately

WHAT YOU WILL NEED
• White 14-count Aida, 32 x 62cm (12½ x 24½in)

DMC STRANDED COTTON (FLOSS)
1 SKEIN

Black 310; white; very dark pewter grey 3799; pewter grey 317; dark steel grey 414; light steel grey 318; pearl grey 415; very light pearl grey 762; black brown 3371; very dark coffee brown 938; dark coffee brown 801; dark golden brown 975; golden brown 3826; med golden brown 976; light golden brown 977; dark brown grey 3787; med brown grey 3022; light brown grey 3023; very light brown grey 3024; dark burnt orange 900; med burnt orange 946; med dark flesh 632; dark flesh 3772; very dark flesh 407; flesh 950; light old gold 676; very light old gold 677; off-white 746; light beige grey 822; med beige grey 644; dark pistachio green 890; dark emerald green 3818; very dark emerald green 909; dark navy blue 823; very dark violet 550; dark violet 327; med violet 552; med brown 433; light brown 434; very light brown 435; tan 436; light tan 437; very light tan 739; light topaz 726; very light antique blue 3752; light antique blue 932

1. Prepare your fabric for work, reading the Techniques section if necessary. Refer to the Stitch Guide on pages 11–13 for how to work the stitches, working the duck design from the centre outwards using the charts on pages 24 and 25.

2. When stitching the design as a picture use two strands of stranded cotton (floss) for all the cross stitch and one strand of stranded cotton (floss) for the backstitch, over one block of the Aida.

3. Work the backstitch detail in stranded cotton (floss) black 310 around the ducks' eyes, beaks and legs, and use white to outline the wing feathers.

4. Refer to the section on Mounting and Framing on page 10 for advice on how to complete your wild duck picture.

Wild Duck Draught Excluder

FINISHED DESIGN SIZE
28 x 79cm (11 x 31in) approximately

WHAT YOU WILL NEED
• Dove grey 16-count Aida (E3251), 43 x 94cm (17 x 37in)
• Heavyweight cotton backing fabric, 40cm x 115cm (½yd x 45in) wide
• Medium-weight iron-on interfacing, 40cm x115cm (½yd x 45in) wide
• Polyester wadding (batting) for filling
• Matching sewing thread

DMC STRANDED COTTON (FLOSS)
Use the thread list for the Wild Duck Picture (left), but you will need two skeins each of off-white 746; light antique blue 932 and very light antique blue 3752, and three skeins each of black 310 and white

1. Prepare your fabric for work, reading the Techniques section if necessary. Refer to the Stitch Guide pages 11–13 for how to work the stitches, working the design from the centre outwards and following the charts.

2. When stitching use three strands of stranded cotton (floss) for the cross stitch and two for the backstitch, over two blocks of Aida.

3. Work the backstitch detail in black 310 to outline the eyes, beaks and legs, and use white to outline the wing feathers.

4. When the design is complete, back with medium-weight iron-on interfacing (see manufacturer's instructions) to strengthen the fabric and to help keep the stitches secure. Using a soft pencil, draw a line all around the design measuring 5cm (2in) from the finished embroidery. Cut away excess fabric along this line.

5. Cut a rectangle of backing fabric, slightly larger than the embroidery. With right sides facing, place the front and back pieces together, then pin and tack (baste) around the edges. Machine stitch the layers together, taking a 1.5cm (⅝in) seam allowance and leaving a 30cm (12in) gap along the bottom edge for turning.

6. Clip into the seams where necessary, then turn through to the right side. Fill the draught excluder with polyester wadding (batting) and then secure the gap with slipstitching.

WILD DUCKS

In the bird world, males tend to be much more colourful than females, and the pochard is no exception with his brick-red head, black breast and grey back. They can be found nesting in tall vegetation around inland stretches of fresh water, whilst the small, timid teal prefer small ponds, which often freeze over in cold weather. The tufted duck, with his white chest and purple-tufted head, has no problems finding food during the cold winter months, as they are one of the most popular ducks to be found in city parks and lakes, where they feed on daily scraps of bread and biscuits. The goldeneye is a winter visitor from Scandinavia and Asia and likes to nest in tree holes near lakes and rivers. Wigeon are more like geese than ducks, as they graze on grass and fly in formations.

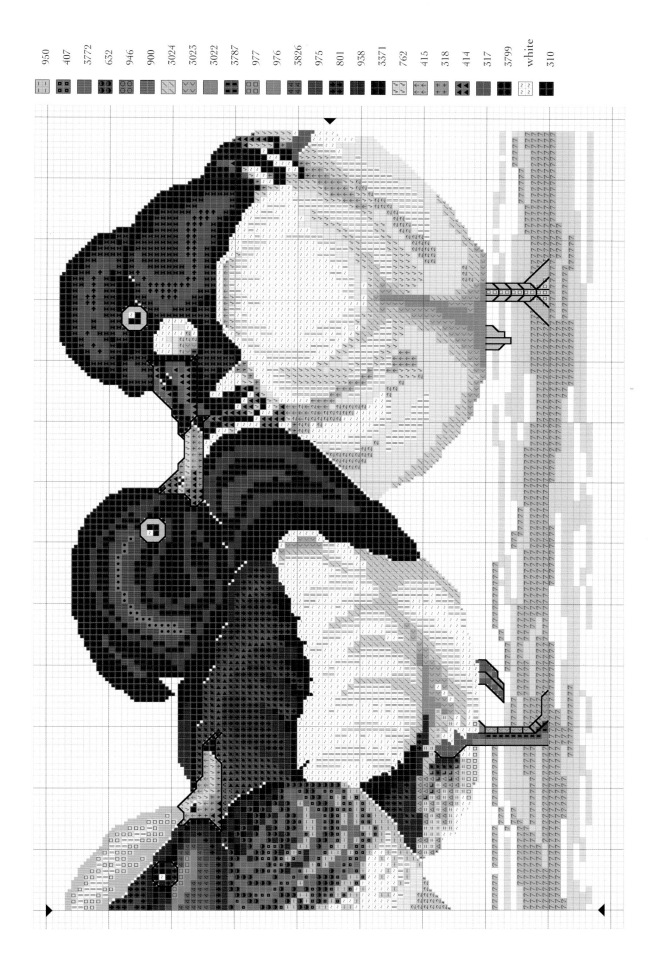

Common Carp Picture

This wonderful design captures the movement of the wild carp as he glides through the water. This magnificent fish is so impressive that no background detail is needed. He is worked in cross stitch, three-quarter cross stitch and backstitch, in a mixture of colours from white and straw, through to deep yellow, olive green and mahogany, which gives his scales the characteristic colourings so reminiscent of the wild carp, and which contrasts superbly against the dark blue Aida.

FINISHED DESIGN SIZE
20 x 33cm (7¾ x 13in) approximately

WHAT YOU WILL NEED
• Cadet blue 14-count Aida, 35 x 48cm (13¾ x 19in)

DMC STRANDED COTTON (FLOSS)
1 SKEIN
Black 310; white; very pale yellow 3823; light pale yellow 745; light straw 3822; med straw 3821; dark straw 3820; med topaz 783; dark topaz 782; very dark topaz 780; light brown 434; med brown 433; dark coffee brown 801; very dark coffee brown 938; black brown 3371; olive green 732; dark olive green 731; very light mocha brown 3033; light mocha brown 3782; med mocha brown 3032; dark mocha brown 3781; med mahogany 301; very light mahogany 402
2 SKEINS
Very dark topaz 781

1. Prepare your fabric for work, reading the Techniques section if necessary. Refer to the Stitch Guide pages 11–13 for how to work the stitches, working from the centre outwards.
2. When stitching the design use two strands of stranded cotton (floss) for the cross stitch and one strand for the backstitch.

3. Once the cross stitching is complete, work the backstitch detail in black 310 around the eye.
4. Refer to Mounting and Framing page 10 for how to complete your picture.

COMMON CARP
The common carp is one of the largest and longest-lived fish found in fresh waters. Although originating from Asia, it is thought that the Romans originally introduced them to Europe as a food source, as carp remains have been found in archaeological digs. This species ranges from the distinctive common carp, with its greenish-brown colour and large uniform scales, to the beautiful golden carp found in ornamental pools.

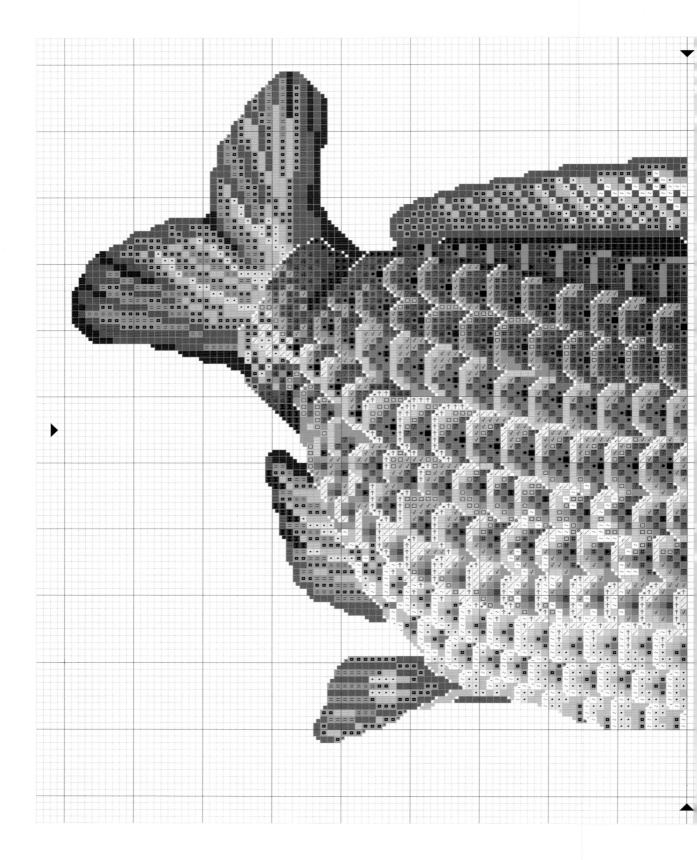

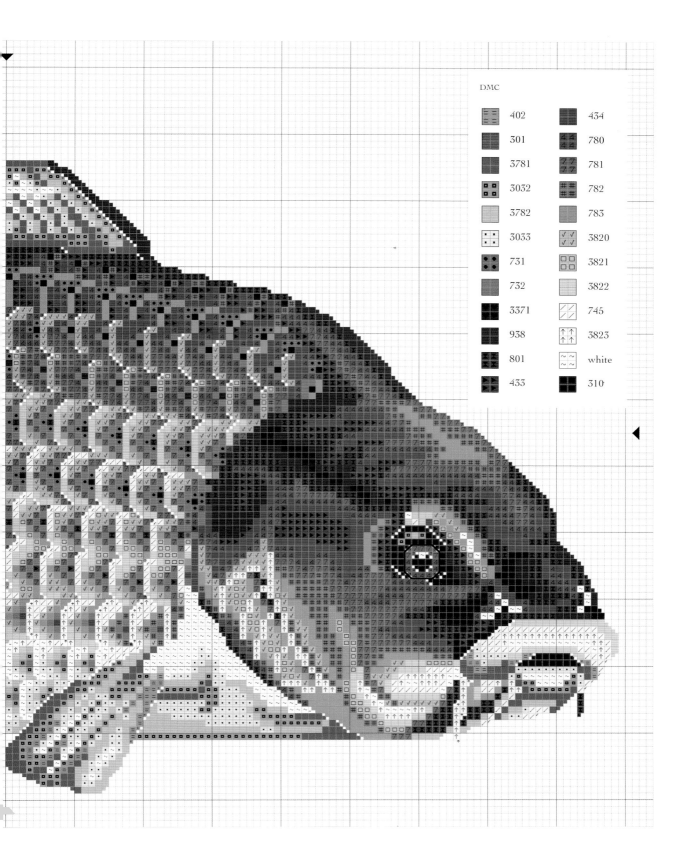

DMC

402		434
301		780
3781		781
3032		782
3782		783
3033		3820
731		3821
732		3822
3371		745
938		3823
801		white
433		310

Dragonflies and Irises

This attractive design is extremely versatile as it is made up from several smaller designs. The waistcoat uses both designs whereas the bell pull uses the larger design only, with delicate dragonflies arranged at random. Different coloured fabrics are used to set off the design which is worked in a mixture of cross stitch, three-quarter cross stitch and backstitch.

Dragonflies and Irises Waistcoat

FINISHED DESIGN SIZE

Large iris design, 7.5 x 20.5cm (3 x 8in) approximately
Small iris design, 5 x 14cm (2 x 5½in) approximately
Dragonfly designs, 5cm (2in) square approximately

WHAT YOU WILL NEED

- A purchased pattern for a waistcoat
- Antique green 28-count Quaker cloth (E3993) or other linen or evenweave fabric (refer to your pattern for fabric requirements)
- Fabric for the back and lining (refer to your pattern for fabric requirements)
- Buttons (refer to your pattern for number required)
- Matching sewing thread

DMC STRANDED COTTON (FLOSS)
1 SKEIN

Irises: White; med yellow green 3347; green 3346; dark green 3345; very dark green 895; light golden yellow 3078; very light topaz 727; light topaz 726; topaz 725; med burnt orange 946; dark coffee brown 938; med golden brown 976; golden brown 3826; dark golden brown 975; dark coffee brown 801; copper 921; pine green 3364; light old gold 676

1 SKEIN

Dragonflies: Black 310; white; light shell grey 453; copper 921; dark coffee brown 801; dark emerald green 3818; med emerald green 911; dark delft 798; dark shell grey 451

1. Lay the pattern pieces for the waistcoat fronts on the fabric to be embroidered and tack (baste) around the shapes with sewing thread. (Note: you may find it easier to stitch the designs on to the fabric before cutting out the waistcoat fronts.)

2. Prepare your fabric for work, reading the Techniques section if necessary. Refer to the Stitch Guide pages 11–13 for how to work the stitches, working the designs from the centre outwards. Use two strands of stranded cotton (floss) for the cross stitch and one strand for the backstitch, worked over two threads of evenweave fabric.

3. Work the reeds and irises first, measuring carefully to make sure the designs are placed correctly, then stitch dragonflies randomly over the waistcoat fronts.

4. Work the backstitch detail in pine green 3364 for the grass stems, dark coffee brown 801 for the rushes and dark shell grey 451 to outline the dragonfly wings.

5. Make up the waistcoat and line it with the lining fabric following the instructions for the purchased paper pattern. Finish by adding buttons which complement the colours of the design, or by making and adding matching fabric-covered buttons.

Dragonflies and Irises Bell Pull

FINISHED DESIGN SIZE
Large iris design, 8 x 21cm (3¼ x 8¼in)
approximately
Dragonflies design, 5cm (2in) square approximately

WHAT YOU WILL NEED
- Platinum 14-count Aida, 28 x 66cm (11 x 26in)
- Cotton backing fabric, 20 x 90cm (¼yd x 36in) wide
- Contrast furnishing braid, 1.5m (1⅝yd)
- Matching sewing thread
- Matching tassel
- Bell pull hanging rod, 12.5cm (4¾in) long
  (available from Framecraft – see Stockists page 127)

DMC STRANDED COTTON (FLOSS)
Use the thread list for the Dragonflies and Irises
Waistcoat (left)

1. Prepare your fabric for work, allowing plenty of excess fabric around the edges. The length of the bell pull hanging rods determines the width of the fabric. The hanging rod used here allows for an 11cm (4¼in) wide strip, and 6mm (¼in) wide furnishing braid. Purchase the rods before you start working the design to ensure that they will be wide enough.

2. Refer to the Stitch Guide pages 11–13 for how to work the stitches, working the designs from the centre outwards. Work the large iris design and the four dragonfly designs following the charts overleaf. Use two strands of stranded cotton (floss) for the cross stitch and one strand for the backstitch.

3. Work the backstitch detail in pine green 3364 for the grass stems, dark coffee brown 801 for

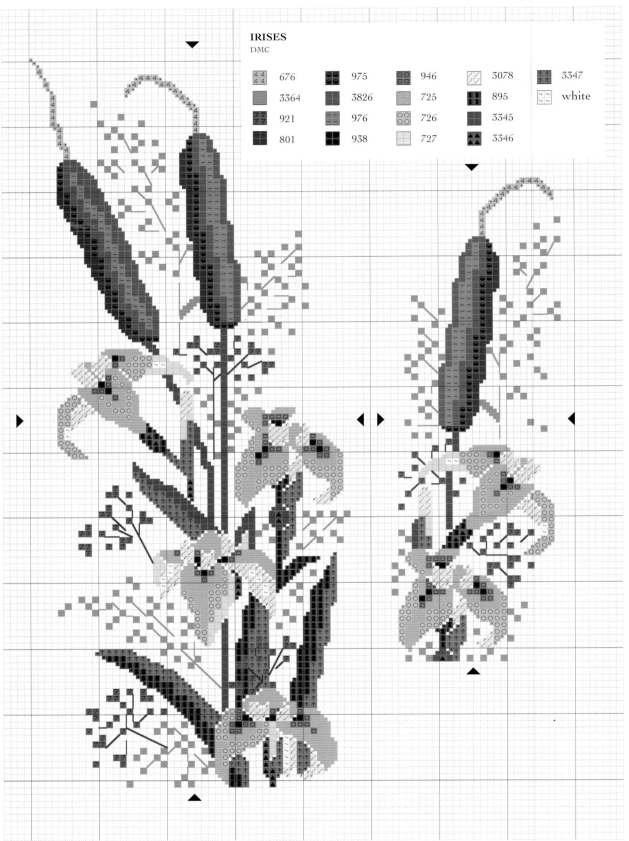

IRISES
DMC

676	975	946	3078	3347
3364	3826	725	895	white
921	976	726	3345	
801	938	727	3346	

the rushes and dark shell grey 451 to outline the dragonfly wings. Once completed, press.

TO MAKE UP THE BELL PULL

1. Mark the correct width and length of the bell pull on the fabric with tacking (basting) lines. Cut the fabric adding 1.5cm (⅝in) along both long and diagonal edges, and 5cm (2in) at the top edge. Press the turnings in place, mitring the corners (fig 15). Cut the backing to the same size but add a 1.5cm (⅝in) turning all round.

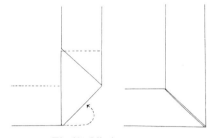

Fig 15 Mitring corners

2. Using matching sewing thread, hand stitch the turnings in place along both long and diagonal edges of the embroidered fabric, then hand stitch furnishing braid around both long and diagonal edges.

3. Position the hanging rod at the top of the strip on the wrong side under the fold of the turnings, then stitch the backing fabric into place. Sew the tassel onto the pointed end of the bell pull.

DRAGONFLIES AND IRISES

Dragonflies were greatly misunderstood by country folk of old who called them 'Horse Stingers' or 'Devil's Darning Needle' because it was thought they contained a lethal sting. The delightful yellow flowers of the iris were thought to be the original inspiration for the fleur-de-lis, a symbol much used in French heraldry, and still used by designers today.

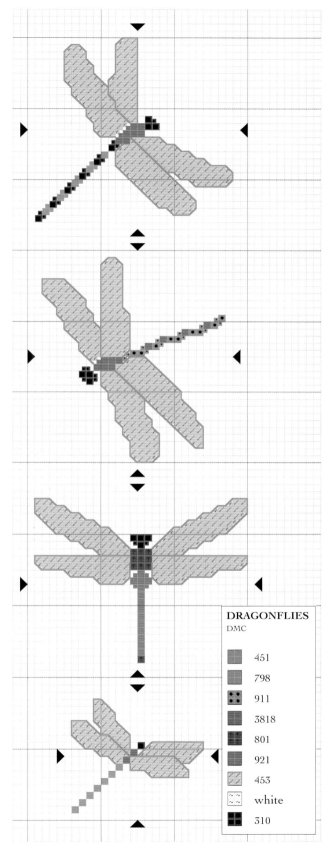

DRAGONFLIES
DMC

	451
	798
	911
	3818
	801
	921
	453
	white
	310

Happy Hippos

This collection of hippo designs, worked in a mixture of cross stitch, three-quarter cross stitch and backstitch, will brighten up accessories for the office or school. The large designs for the note holder and money-box are worked on 14-count Aida, finished off with a simple cross stitch border. A handy key ring contains one small hippo design while the row of small hippos on the ruler are worked on perforated paper.

Hippo Note Holder

FINISHED DESIGN SIZE
Each large hippo 7cm (2¾in) square approximately

WHAT YOU WILL NEED
- White 14-count Aida, 23 x 43cm (9 x 17in)
- Matching sewing thread
- Note holder for embroidery (available from Framecraft – see Stockists page 127)

DMC STRANDED COTTON (FLOSS)
1 SKEIN
Black 310; white; very dark pewter grey 3799; dark pewter grey 413; pewter grey 317; dark steel grey 414; light flesh 754; flesh 353; light coral 352; coral 351; very light tan 738; med antique blue 931; light antique blue 932; dark coffee brown 801

1. Prepare your fabric for work, reading the Techniques section if necessary. To work out where to place the hippo designs for stitching, measure the sides of your note holder (the one we used has 10cm (4in) square sides), then tack (baste) the outlines of three squares in a row, to the correct measurements, spacing them equally along the rectangle of Aida.
2. Refer to the Stitch Guide pages 11–13 for how to work the stitches, working the three large hippo designs, one each at the centre of each square from the centre outwards. Use two strands of stranded cotton (floss) for the cross stitch and one strand for the backstitch. Work the backstitch detail in black 310 to outline the eyes.
3. Complete the designs by adding a cross stitch border, 6mm (¼in) in from the tacked (basted) lines. The border consists of two rows of cross stitches on alternate blocks. Use med antique blue 931 to work the outer border of crosses, then work the inner border inside the first.
4. To complete your note holder, follow the manufacturer's instructions.

Hippo Ruler

FINISHED DESIGN SIZE
Each small hippo, 2.5 x 3.5cm (1 x 1½in)

WHAT YOU WILL NEED
- Ruler complete with perforated paper (available from Framecraft – see Stockists page 127)

DMC STRANDED COTTON (FLOSS)
Use the thread list for the Hippo Note Holder (left) but omit the white, light flesh 754 and med antique blue 931

1. Prepare your fabric for work, reading the Techniques section if necessary. Refer to the Stitch Guide pages 11–13 for how to work the stitches, working the design from the centre outwards.

2. When stitching the designs follow the chart and work the three small hippo designs as shown in the photograph on page 35. Use one strand of stranded cotton (floss) for the cross stitch and backstitch. Work the backstitch detail in black 310 to outline the eyes and bodies.

3. To complete your ruler, follow the manufacturer's instructions.

Hippo Money-Box

FINISHED DESIGN SIZE
Each large hippo 7cm (2¾in) square approximately

WHAT YOU WILL NEED
- Cadet blue 14-count Aida, 23 x 33cm (9 x 13in)
- Matching sewing thread
- Money-box holder for embroidery (available from Framecraft – see Stockists page 127)

DMC STRANDED COTTON (FLOSS)
Use the thread list for the Hippo Note Holder on page 34

1. Prepare your fabric for work, reading the Techniques section if necessary. To work out where to place the two large hippo designs for stitching, measure the frame of the money-box – ours was 10 x 20cm (4 x 8in) – then tack (baste) a rectangle to the correct measurements. Refer to the Stitch Guide pages 11–13 for the stitches, following the chart and working the designs from the centre outwards.

2. When stitching the design use two strands of stranded cotton (floss) for the cross stitch and one strand for the backstitch. Work the backstitch detail in black 310 to outline the eyes and use dark coffee brown 801 for the teeth and mouth area.

3. Complete the design by adding a cross stitch border, consisting of two rows of cross stitches on alternate blocks. Use light antique blue 932 to work the outer border of crosses, 6mm (¼in) in from the tacked (basted) lines, then work the inner border inside the first.

4. To complete your money-box, follow the manufacturer's instructions.

Hippo Key Ring

FINISHED DESIGN SIZE
Each small hippo 2.5 x 3.5cm (1 x 1⅜in)

WHAT YOU WILL NEED
- White 14-count Aida, 15cm (6in) square
- Key ring for embroidery (available from Framecraft – see Stockists page 127)

DMC STRANDED COTTON (FLOSS)
Use the thread list for the Hippo Note Holder on page 34 but omit the white, light flesh 754 and med antique blue 931

1. Prepare your fabric for work, reading the Techniques section if necessary. Refer to the Stitch Guide pages 11–13 for the stitches, working the design from the centre outwards.

2. When stitching the design follow the chart. Use two strands of stranded cotton (floss) for the cross stitch and one strand for the backstitch. Work the backstitch detail in black 310 to outline the eyes and body.

3. To complete your key ring follow the manufacturer's instructions.

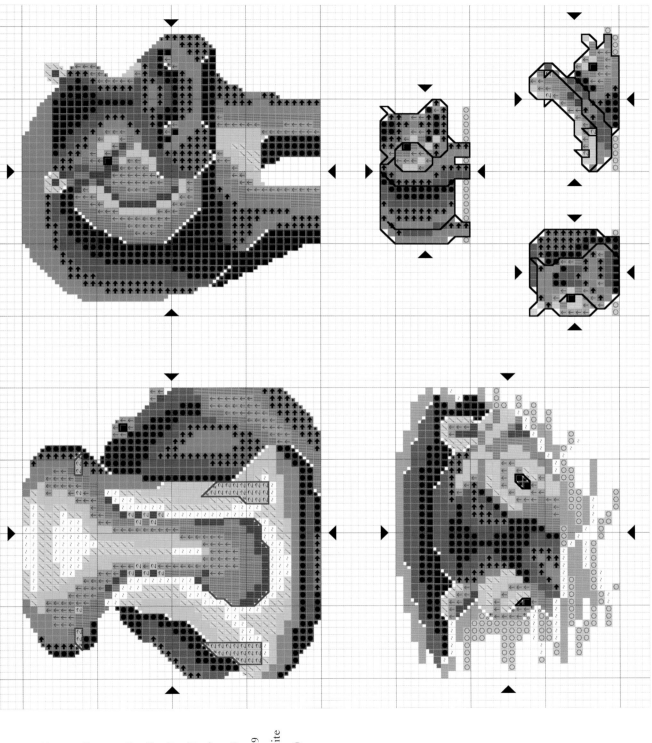

801 932 931 738 351 352 353 754 414 317 413 3799 white 310

Flamingos Picture

These graceful looking birds with their long thin legs, large bodies and slender necks, look like ballet dancers wearing fluffy, pale pink tutus. The ice blue linen evenweave fabric provides a delicate contrast to the subtle pale pink flamingos, and the muted blues of the soda lake. This design uses cross stitch, three-quarter cross stitch and backstitch, worked on a 28-count evenweave fabric, but the design would be the same size if worked on a 14-count Aida.

FINISHED DESIGN SIZE
20.5 x 28cm (8 x 11in) approximately

WHAT YOU WILL NEED
• Ice blue 28-count Annabelle (E3240), 35.5 x 43cm (14 x 17in)

DMC STRANDED COTTON (FLOSS)
1 SKEIN
Black 310; white; very light peach flesh 948; light peach flesh 754; peach flesh 353; light coral 352; coral 351; med coral 350; dark coral 349; very dark coral red 817; light brown 434; dark coffee brown 801; dark coffee brown 938; pale yellow 744; very dark flesh 3064; med flesh 3773; flesh 950; very dark antique blue 3750; med antique blue 931; light antique blue 932; very light antique blue 3752; dark green grey 3051; med green grey 3052; light hazelnut brown 422; dark hazelnut brown 420; very dark hazelnut brown 869
2 SKEINS
Dark antique blue 930

1. Prepare your fabric for work, reading the Techniques section if necessary. Refer to the Stitch Guide pages 11–13 for the stitches, working the design from the centre outwards.
2. When stitching the design use two strands of stranded cotton (floss) for the cross stitch and one for the backstitch, over two threads.

3. Work the backstitch detail in dark coffee brown 938 for the eyes and beaks, and dark coffee brown 801 to outline the flamingos' legs.
4. Refer to Mounting and Framing page 10 for how to complete your picture.

GREATER FLAMINGO
Flocks of flamingos gather at Africa's salty soda lakes to feed. Their long legs enable the birds to wade in deep water, but when the weather becomes hot, the water evaporates, leaving a steaming potion of concentrated soda. The crystallised salts in the water harden and become encrusted around the thin legs of some young birds, making it impossible to make the long migration flights. Flamingos are not adapted very well to flight; with their long necks outstretched and their legs trailing behind them, they find it difficult to manoeuvre and are vulnerable to attack. Because of this the long migration journeys take place at night.

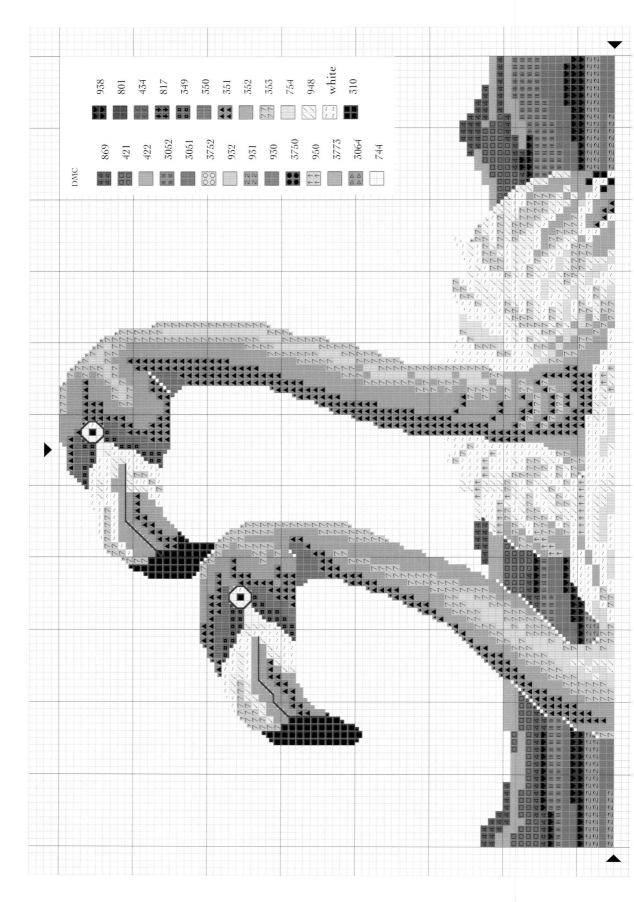

DMC												
938	801	434	817	349	350	351	352	353	754	948	white	310
869	421	422	3052	3051	3752	932	931	930	3750	950	3773	3064	744

Waterside Flowers

Wild flowers were the inspiration for this design worked in cross stitch, three-quarter cross stitch, backstitch and French knots. The pink and purple shades of the loosestrife form a rich contrast against the pale pink water-mint petals, the cream meadowsweet and the white-flowered grass of Parnassus. Each corner of the table-cloth is decorated with the garland, whilst smaller designs are used for the napkins, tray and coasters.

Floral Table-Cloth

FINISHED DESIGN SIZE
Large floral motif (design A), 23 x 23 x 33cm
(9 x 9 x 13in)
Medium floral motif (design B), 9cm (3½in) diameter
approximately

WHAT YOU WILL NEED
- Sage 27-count Linda (E1235) or other linen or evenweave fabric, 1.10m (1¼yd) square
- Matching sewing thread

DMC STRANDED COTTON (FLOSS)
1 SKEIN
White; very light pistachio green 369; light pistachio green 368; topaz 725; very light topaz 727; light plum 3607; med plum 917; dark plum 915; dark coffee brown 801; very dark shell pink 221; dark shell pink 3721; light dusty rose 963; very light dusty rose 3716; mauve 3687; med yellow green 3347; hunter green 3346; dark hunter green 3345; forest green 989; med forest green 988; very dark forest green 986; very light old gold 677
2 SKEINS
Off-white 746

1. Prepare your fabric for work, reading the Techniques section if necessary. Neaten the raw edges of the cloth by pressing up a 1.5cm (⅝in) turning, and then stitch the hem in place. Hand embroider to make a decorative hem if you wish. This hemming could be done after the embroidery if you prefer.

2. Refer to the Stitch Guide pages 11–13 for how to work the stitches. Using two strands of stranded cotton (floss) for the cross stitch over two threads of evenweave fabric, work the large floral motif (design A, page 47) in two opposite corners of the table-cloth, working the design from the centre outwards (or the corners if you prefer). Then work the medium floral motif (design B, page 46) in the other two corners. Measure carefully to make sure the designs are placed correctly in the corners. If you wish, the cream meadowsweet flowers can be worked in French knots instead of cross stitch, using two strands of very light old gold 677 and off-white 746.

3. Work the backstitch detail over two threads of evenweave fabric, using two strands of stranded cotton (floss) in very dark shell pink 221 for the stalks of the cream meadowsweet flowers, and very dark forest green 986 for the stalks of the pale pink water-mint flowers. Use one strand of light pistachio green 368 to work the backstitch around the white flower petals.

The Floral Table-cloth with its two pretty waterside flowers designs

Floral Coasters

FINISHED DESIGN SIZE
Small floral motif (design C), 6cm (2¼in) square
approximately

WHAT YOU WILL NEED FOR FOUR COASTERS
- Sage 27-count Linda (E1235) or other linen or evenweave fabric, 28cm (11in) square
- Four coasters for needlework (available from Framecraft – see Stockists page 127)

DMC STRANDED COTTON (FLOSS)
Use the thread list for the Floral Tray (right) but omit topaz 725

1. Prepare your fabric for work, reading the Techniques section if necessary. Refer to the Stitch Guide pages 11–13 for the stitches, working the designs from the centre outwards.
2. Work four of the small floral motifs (design C) from the chart on page 46, one in each quarter of the linen square, using two strands of stranded cotton (floss) for the cross stitch over two threads of evenweave fabric.

3. Work the backstitch detail over two threads of fabric, using two strands of stranded cotton (floss) in very dark shell pink 221 for the stalks of the ·cream meadowsweet flowers. Use one strand of light pistachio green 368 for the backstitch around the white flower petals.
4. To complete your coasters, follow the manufacturer's instructions.

Floral Tray

FINISHED DESIGN SIZE
Medium floral motif (design B), 9cm (3½in) diameter
approximately

WHAT YOU WILL NEED
- Sage 27-count Linda (E1235) or other linen or evenweave fabric, 33cm (13in) square
- Circular tray for embroidery (available from Framecraft – see Stockists page 127)

DMC STRANDED COTTON (FLOSS)
1 SKEIN
White; very light pistachio green 369; light pistachio green 368; topaz 725; very light topaz 727; light plum 3607; med plum 917; dark plum 915; dark coffee brown 801; very dark shell pink 221; dark shell pink 3721; dark hunter green 3345; off-white 746; very light old gold 677

1. Prepare your fabric for work, reading the Techniques section if necessary. Refer to the Stitch Guide pages 11–13 for how to work the stitches, working the medium-sized floral motif (design B) from the centre outwards and using the chart on page 46.

2. When stitching the design use two strands of stranded cotton (floss) for the cross stitch, worked over two threads of evenweave fabric.

3. Work the backstitch detail over two threads of evenweave fabric, using two strands of stranded cotton (floss) in very dark shell pink 221 for the stalks of the cream meadowsweet flowers. Use one strand of light pistachio green 368 to work the backstitch around the white flower petals.

4. To complete your tray, follow the manufacturer's instructions.

Floral Napkins

FINISHED DESIGN SIZE
Small floral motif (design C), 6cm (2¼in) square approximately

WHAT YOU WILL NEED FOR EACH NAPKIN
• Sage 27-count Linda (E1235) or other linen or evenweave fabric, 33cm (13in) square
• Matching sewing thread

DMC STRANDED COTTON (FLOSS)
Use the thread list for the Floral Tray (page 44) but omit topaz 725

1. Prepare your fabric for work, reading the Techniques section if necessary. Refer to the Stitch Guide pages 11–13 for how to work the stitches. Neaten the raw edges of each napkin by pressing up a 1cm (⅜in) turning, and then stitch the hem in place. Hand embroider to make a decorative hem if you wish.

2. Work the small floral motif (design C) from the chart on page 46 at the bottom right-hand corner of each napkin, measuring carefully to make sure the design is placed correctly. Use two strands of stranded cotton (floss) for the cross stitch, worked over two threads of evenweave fabric. If you wish, the cream meadowsweet flowers can be worked in French knots instead of cross stitch, using two strands of very light old gold 677 and off-white 746.

3. Work the backstitch detail over two threads of evenweave fabric, using two strands of stranded cotton (floss) in very dark shell pink 221 for the stalks of the cream meadowsweet flowers. Use one strand of light pistachio green 368 to work the backstitch around the white flower petals.

WATERSIDE FLOWERS
Wild flowers and herbs have long been used in cooking and as medicinal remedies. Meadowsweet or 'mede sweete' was used to flavour mead and to ease pain and reduce fever. The grass of Parnassus was used to treat liver disorders and to aid digestion. Water-mint was an early form of smelling salts and air freshener, and the juice from the purple loose-strife was used for tanning leather.

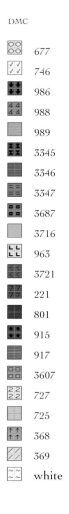

DMC

677
746
986
988
989
3345
3346
3347
3687
3716
963
3721
221
801
915
917
3607
727
725
368
369
white

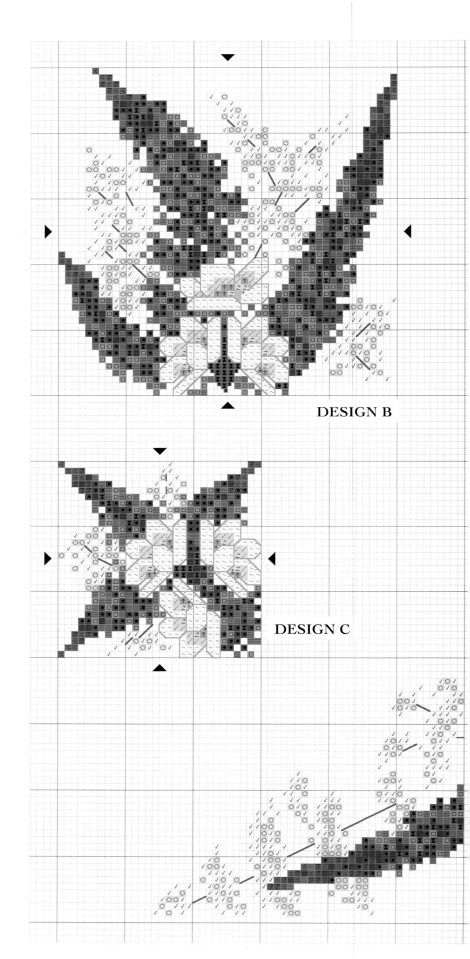

DESIGN B

DESIGN C

DESIGN A

Rivers & Estuaries

This selection of projects is chosen from the wildlife that can be found as a river follows its journey from a trickling stream, into a fast-flowing current, finally reaching its journey's end at the estuary and seashore.

You may think that magnificent Camargue horses, pictured here, are an unusual animal to find along the water's edge, but these horses run wild through the swampland and marshes of the Camargue region in southern France and make the perfect subject for a picture.

You will be spoilt for choice as you try to decide which designs to work. There are colourful kingfishers – the blue-green common kingfisher and more exotic kingfishers – ideal for creating colourful cushions and a bell pull. Majestic swans decorate a beautiful dressing-table set, worked on 22-count evenweave fabric with silk and metallic threads. Leaping salmon work their way up river against the flow of the water to reach their breeding grounds. Hessian (jute) and felt transform this image into a stunning wall hanging, with tiny glass beads for the foaming water. Further down river there is a brown bear on the look-out for salmon, making an impressive subject for a picture.

As the river finally opens out at its journey's end, it reaches the estuary and the seashore, where fresh and tidal salt waters mix. An estuary clock captures a simple estuary scene, surrounded by bunches of pretty pink sea-pea flowers, and to finish there is a beautiful cormorant picture and a cushion framed with a knotted rope border.

Colourful Kingfishers

These beautiful birds come in many different colours but here in Britain we are most familiar with the brilliant blue common kingfisher, though they are a rare sight. This striking design shows the pied, blue-breasted, rufous-backed and common kingfishers. The birds are worked as a group for the bell pull, and in pairs for the two cushions, using a mixture of cross stitch, three-quarter cross stitch, backstitch and French knots, on 14-count Aida in a variety of colours.

Kingfisher Bell Pull

FINISHED DESIGN SIZE
13 x 47cm (5 x 18½in) approximately

WHAT YOU WILL NEED
- Antique green 14-count Aida, 28 x 66cm (11 x 26in)
- Cotton backing fabric, 30 x 90cm (⅜yd x 36in) wide
- Bell pull hanging rod, 20cm (8in) long
- Contrast furnishing braid, 1.5m (1⅝yd)
- Matching sewing thread

DMC STRANDED COTTON (FLOSS)
For your convenience, the colours for each bird and background have been listed separately. Although some colour shades are listed more than once, you will only need 1 skein of each colour to stitch the complete bell pull

1 SKEIN
Pied kingfisher: Black 310; white; very light pearl grey 762; pearl grey 415; light steel grey 318; dark steel grey 414; pewter grey 317; dark pewter grey 413; very dark pewter grey 3799; very dark mahogany 300; dark mahogany 400

Blue-breasted kingfisher: Black 310; white; very light pearl grey 762; pearl grey 415; light steel grey 318; dark steel grey 414; pewter grey 317; dark pewter grey 413; very dark pewter grey 3799; med burnt orange 946; dark peacock blue 806; med electric blue 996; very dark mahogany 300; dark coral 349; light baby blue 3325; very light baby blue 775; dark mahogany 400

Rufous-backed kingfisher: Black 310; white; med burnt orange 946; very dark mahogany 300; dark coral 349; very dark coral red 817; very dark garnet 902; very dark rose 326; dark rose 309; rose 335; copper 921; tangerine 740; med tangerine 741; light tangerine 742; med yellow 743; pale yellow 744; light pale yellow 745; dark mahogany 400

Common kingfisher: Black 310; white; pewter grey 317; dark pewter grey 413; very dark pewter grey 3799; med burnt orange 946; dark turquoise 3808; dark aquamarine 991; aquamarine 3814; aquamarine 992; light aquamarine 993; dark peacock blue 806; med electric blue 996; very light orange spice 3825; light orange spice 722; med orange spice 721; dark orange spice 720; very dark mahogany 300; light baby blue 3325; dark mahogany 400

Foliage: White; very dark mahogany 300; coral 351; med coral 350; dark coral 349; very dark coral red 817; med yellow 743; light pale yellow 745; dark moss green 580; moss green 581; light moss green 3819; med beige brown 840; light beige brown 841; very light beige brown 842

Border: White; light tangerine 742; dark moss green 580; moss green 581; light moss green 3819

1. Prepare your fabric for work, reading the Techniques section if necessary and allowing plenty of excess fabric around the edges. The length of the bell pull hanging rod determines the width of the fabric. The hanging rod used here allows for a 19cm (7½in) wide strip and 6mm (¼in) wide braid. Purchase the rod before you start working the design to ensure that it will be wide enough.

2. Refer to the Stitch Guide pages 11–13 for how to work the stitches, working the design from the centre outwards.

3. When stitching the design use two strands of stranded cotton (floss) for the cross stitch and one strand for the backstitch and French knots. Work the backstitch detail in black 310 around the beaks and eyes, and use very dark mahogany 300 for the flower stamens. Use white to work a French knot for the highlight in each eye. When you have completed the stitching, press.

TO MAKE UP THE BELL PULL

1. Mark the correct width and length of the bell pull on to the fabric with tacking (basting) lines. Cut the fabric along these lines adding 1.5cm (⅝in) along the side and bottom edges and 5cm (2in) at the top edge. Press the turnings in place. Cut the cotton backing fabric to the same size but add 1.5cm (⅝in) turnings all the way round.

2. Hand stitch the turnings in place along the side and bottom edges of the embroidered fabric, then hand stitch furnishing braid around the turned edges. Position the hanging rod at the top of the strip, on the wrong side under the fold of the turnings, then stitch the backing fabric into place to finish.

Left: The eye-catching kingfishers are worked as a group to create this unusual bell pull. They can also be worked in pairs to make attractive cushions (see instructions overleaf)

Kingfisher Cushions

FINISHED DESIGN SIZE
Design and border, 30cm (11¾in) square
approximately

WHAT YOU WILL NEED FOR ONE CUSHION
- Lemon or cream 14-count Aida, 50cm (20in) square
- Cotton fabric for backing and frill, 1m x 115cm (1⅛yd x 45in) wide
- Matching sewing thread
- Square cushion pad to fit

DMC STRANDED COTTON (FLOSS)
Use the thread list for the Kingfisher Bell Pull on page 50. Although some colour shades are listed more than once, you will only need 1 skein of each colour for each cushion

1. Prepare your fabric for work, reading the Techniques section if necessary. Use a soft pencil to mark a 38cm (15in) square at the centre of the Aida fabric. The border will be worked 4cm (1¾in) below the marked pencil line, while the birds of your choice are worked in opposite corners 2.5cm (1in) from the border (see photograph). Refer to the Stitch Guide pages 11–13 for how to work the stitches, working the birds from the centre outwards (or from the corners inwards if you prefer).

2. Following the charts on pages 54–55, work the designs, using two strands of stranded cotton (floss) for the cross stitch and one strand for the backstitch and French knots. Work the backstitch detail in black 310 around the beaks and eyes, and use very dark mahogany 300 for the flower stamens. Use white to work a French knot for the highlight in each eye.

3. When working the border, omit working the white squares. For the border on the lemon cushion, dark coral 349 is used to replace light tangerine 742.

TO MAKE UP THE CUSHION

1. For the cushion front, carefully cut away the excess fabric along the marked pencil line,
leaving an embroidered square with a 1.5cm (⅝in) seam allowance.

2. For the cushion backs, cut two pieces of cotton fabric 25.5 x 38cm (10 x 15in), then take each rectangle and hem along one long edge.

3. To make the frill, cut enough 12cm (4¾in) wide strips along the length of the cotton fabric to give a finished length of 2.9m (3⅛yd). With right sides facing, stitch the fabric strips together along the short edges to form a circle. Press the seams open. Fold the strip in half so that the long edges meet, enclosing the raw edges of the short seams (fig 16), then press.

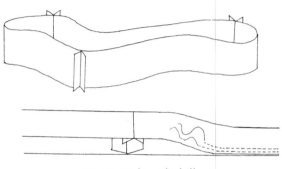

Fig 16 Making the frill

4. Run two rows of gathering threads along the raw edges of the frill fabric. Pull up the gathering thread until the frill is the right length, then distribute the gathers evenly. With the embroidered fabric facing upwards, place the frill around the outer edge of the cushion front, so that raw edges face outwards. Distribute the gathers evenly, then pin, tack (baste) and stitch in place.

5. Lay the embroidered fabric face upwards on a flat surface. With right sides facing down, lay the two rectangles of the cushion back over the front so that all raw edges match and the hemmed edges overlap at the centre. Pin, tack (baste) and machine stitch along the stitching line and through all layers of fabric. Neaten the raw edges, then turn the cover through to the right side and insert the cushion pad.

DMC

⁺⁺ / ⁺⁺	842
	841
	840
	400
	3819
	581
	580
	775
	3325
##	745
			744
○○	743
	742
44 / 44	741
	740
	921
	335
	309
	326
	902
	817
	349
	350
LL	351
	300
	720
◧◧	721
	722
○○	3825
	996
ZZ	806
	993
<<	992
	3814
	991
	3808
	946
	3799
	413
◀◀	317
	414
↑↑	318
	415
	762
~~	white
	310

PIED
KINGFISHER

BLUE-BREASTED
KINGFISHER

RUFOUS-BACKED
KINGFISHER

COMMON
KINGFISHER

Swan Dressing-Table Set

This beautiful design is worked in cross stitch and backstitch on 22-count evenweave fabric. The gracefulness of the swan is highlighted by the subtle shades of grey, blue and white, mixed with silver and gold metallic threads. You could work the design as a picture, on 14-count Aida, with the flowers on the grasses replaced with tiny gold beads.

FINISHED DESIGN SIZES
Brush, 7 x 10cm (2¾ x 4in) approximately
Mirror, 6.5 x 8cm (2½ x 3¼in) approximately
Powder puff, 7cm (2¾in) diameter approximately

WHAT YOU WILL NEED
- White 22-count Hardanger, 28cm (11in) square for the mirror; 23cm (9in) square for the brush; and 18cm (7in) square for the powder puff
- Dressing-table set and powder puff for embroidery (available from Framecraft – see Stockists page 127)

DMC STRANDED COTTON (FLOSS)
1 SKEIN
Black 310; white; very light pearl grey 762; pearl grey 415; light steel grey 318; light tangerine 742; light shell grey 453; med shell grey 452; dark shell grey 451; very light ash grey 535; golden olive 832

DMC METALLIC STRANDED COTTON (FLOSS)
1 SKEIN
Gold 1001; silver 1000

1. Prepare your fabric for work, reading the Techniques section if necessary. Refer to the Stitch Guide pages 11–13 for the stitches, working from the centre outwards. Work the whole design for the mirror. For the brush, work the swan and two cygnets (omitting the upturned cygnet at the bottom) and the background foliage. For the powder puff, work the swan, one cygnet and the background foliage.

2. When stitching the design use two strands of stranded cotton (floss) for the cross stitch and one strand for the backstitch. For the adult swan, work the areas of white cross stitch by using one strand each of white and silver mixed together. Work the cygnets using white.

3. Work the backstitch detail in black 310 for the beak and gold 1001 for the grass stems and water ripples.

4. To complete the set, follow the manufacturer's instructions for mounting embroidery in the brush, mirror and powder puff.

SWANS
The placid, graceful appearance of the swan is very deceptive and hides their bullying behaviour. In the breeding season, the male aggressively defends his territory. Swans lay their eggs in huge nests and when the cygnets hatch, the female will often carry them through the water on her back.

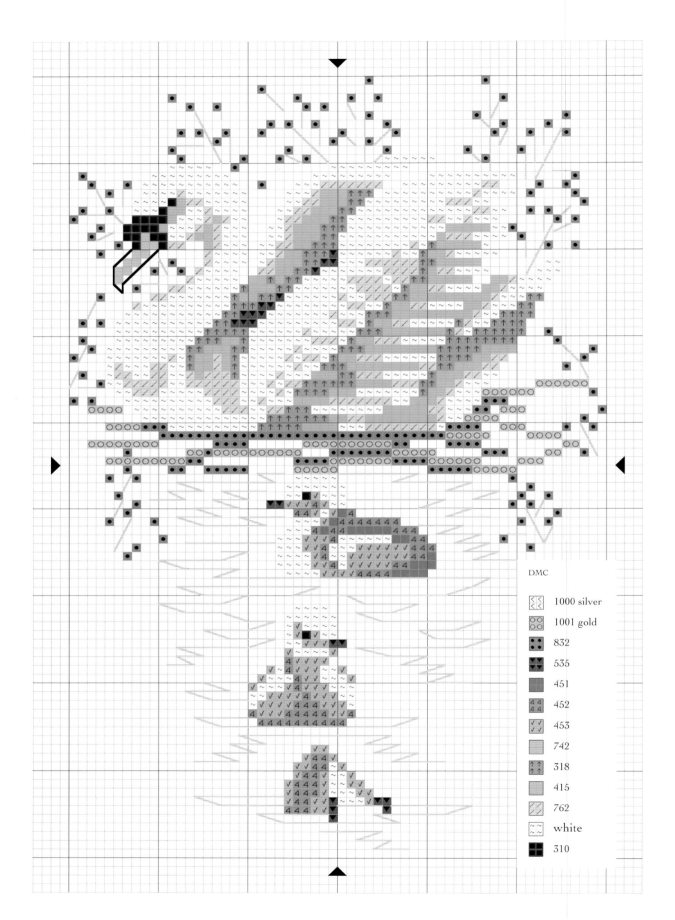

DMC

1000 silver
1001 gold
832
535
451
452
453
742
318
415
762
white
310

Camargue Horses Picture

This ambitious design captures the spirit of the beautiful white Camargue horses which run wild in the swampland of the Rhône delta in France. A combination of cross stitch, three-quarter cross stitch and backstitch are used to create the stunning detail of these magnificent creatures worked on a soft blue 28-count evenweave fabric (see photograph on page 48). The design would be the same size if worked on a 14-count Aida.

FINISHED DESIGN SIZE
35 x 37cm (13¾ x 14½in) approximately

WHAT YOU WILL NEED
• Ice blue 28-count evenweave Annabelle (E3240), 50cm (20in) square

DMC STRANDED COTTON (FLOSS)
1 SKEIN
Black 310; white; very dark beige grey 640; dark beige grey 3790; dark brown grey 3787; very dark brown grey 3021; very dark pewter grey 3799; flesh 950; med flesh 3773; light olive green 734; med olive green 733; olive green 732; dark olive green 731; very dark golden olive 829; light avocado green 470; avocado green 469; med avocado green 937; very dark avocado green 936; light blue green 504; med blue green 503; blue green 502; very light antique blue 3753; very light antique blue 3752; black brown 3371; green grey 3053; med green grey 3052; dark green grey 3051
2 SKEINS
Light beige grey 822; med beige grey 644; dark beige grey 642; black avocado green 934

1. Prepare your fabric for work, reading the Techniques section if necessary. Refer to the Stitch Guide pages 11–13 for how to work the stitches, working the design from the centre outwards.

2. When stitching the design use two strands of stranded cotton (floss) for the cross stitch and one strand for the backstitch, worked over two threads of evenweave fabric.

3. Work the backstitch detail in black stranded cotton (floss) 310 around the eye of the large horse in the foreground.

4. Refer to Mounting and Framing page 10 for how to complete your picture.

CAMARGUE HORSES
These beautiful creatures attract horse lovers and tourists from all over the world to the Camargue region of France, to view them in their natural habitat. This has ensured that the 'manades' or herds still inhabit the swamplands which is their heritage. They are often called 'horses of the sea', because of their foamy white coats reminiscent of 'white horses' at sea. However, the foals are born grey, black or mottled brown and only turn to their recognisable white when they grow older.

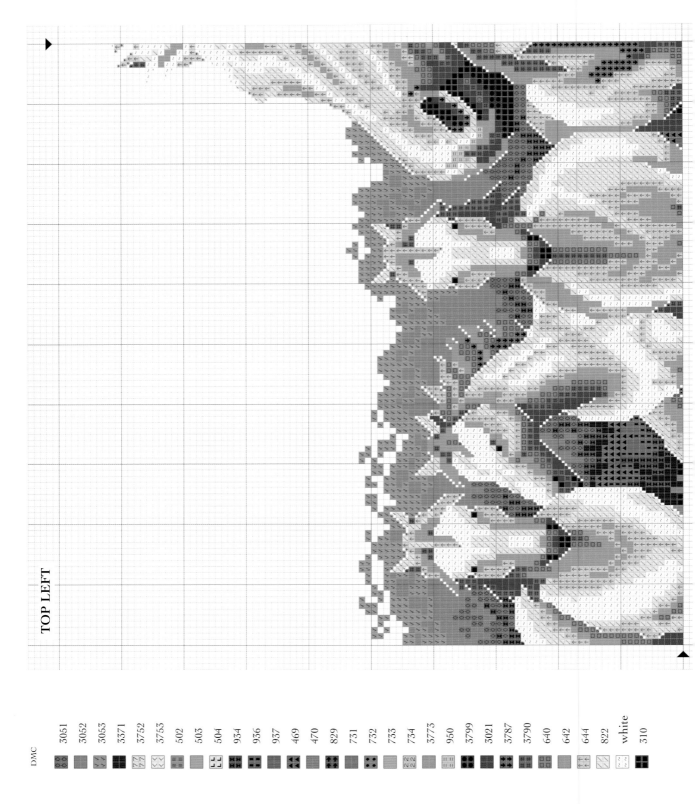

TOP LEFT

DMC 3051 3052 3053 3371 3752 3753 502 503 504 934 936 957 469 470 829 731 732 733 734 3773 950 3799 3021 3787 3790 640 642 644 822 white 310

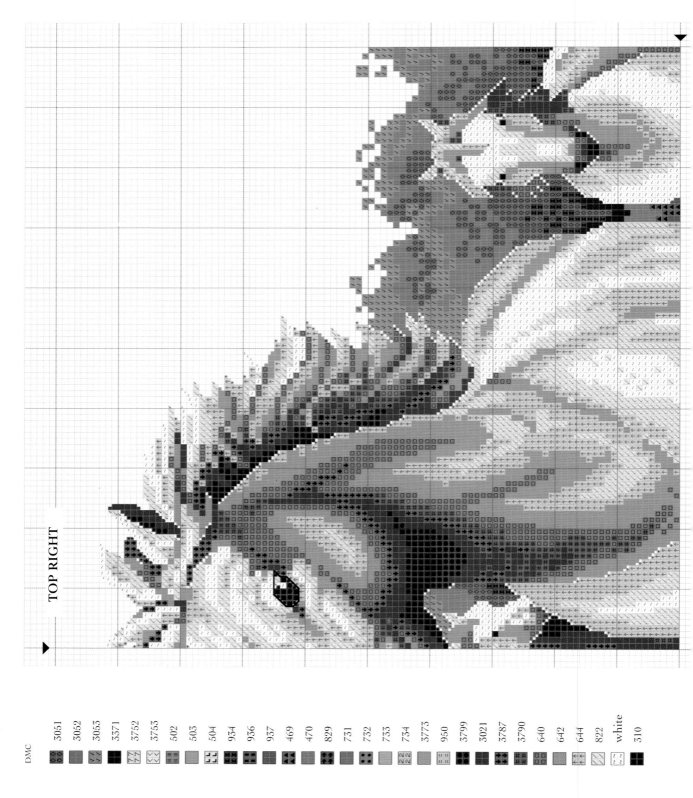

TOP RIGHT

DMC	3051	3052	3053	3371	3752	3753	502	503	504	934	936	937	469	470	829	731	732	733	734	3773	950	3799	3021	3787	3790	640	642	644	822	white	310

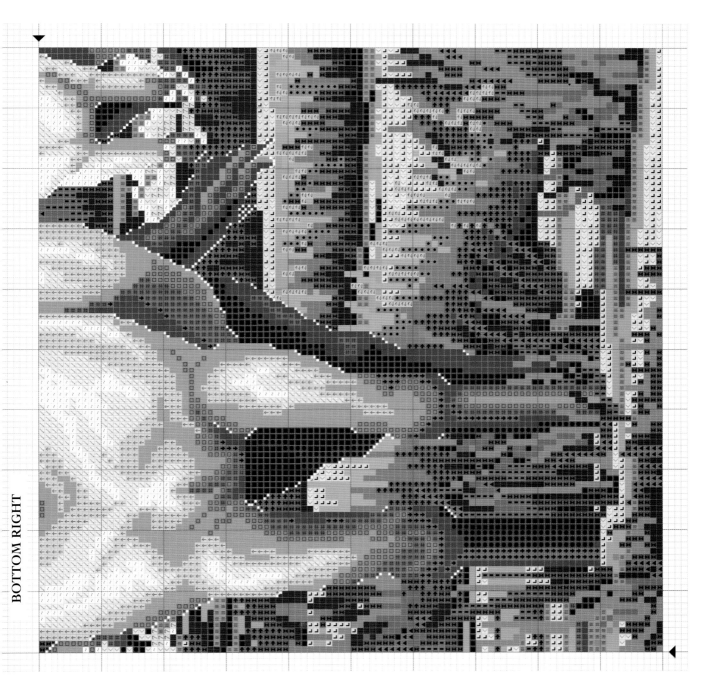

BOTTOM RIGHT

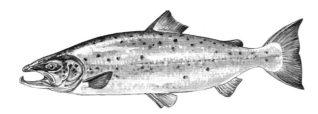

Leaping Salmon Wall Hanging

As this salmon leaps through the rapids, splashes of water are highlighted with sparkling glass beads. The silvery-pink tones of the salmon and the white foaming water are worked in cross stitch, three-quarter stitch and backstitch detail, against a sage green background.

FINISHED DESIGN SIZE
21 x 30.5cm (8¼ x 12in) approximately

WHAT YOU WILL NEED
- Sage 14-count Aida, 33 x 46cm (13 x 18in)
- Dark green felt, 34 x 50cm (13½ x 20in)
- Hessian (jute), 33 x 38cm (13 x 15in)
- Hanging rod or stick, 48cm (19in) long
- Matching sewing threads

DMC STRANDED COTTON (FLOSS)
1 SKEIN
Black 310; hint of grey 762; pearl grey 415; light steel grey 318; dark steel grey 414; med dark flesh 632; dark flesh 3772; very dark flesh 3064; dark green grey 3051; med green grey 3052; very light ash grey 535; dark shell grey 451; med shell grey 452; dark saffron yellow 725; med saffron yellow 726; very light antique blue 3753; very light antique blue 3752; light antique blue 932; med antique blue 931; blue green 502; dark blue green 501; very dark blue green 500; med olive green 733; olive green 732; dark old gold 680; med old gold 729; light old gold 676; very light old gold 677; black brown 3371; dark coffee brown 938; dark coffee brown 801; very light baby blue 3756 (optional)
2 SKEINS
White
MILL HILL BEADS
Glass seed beads, 3 packs, crystal 00161 (optional)

1. Prepare your fabric for work, reading the Techniques section if necessary. Refer to the Stitch Guide pages 11–13 for how to work the stitches and attach the beads, working the design from the centre outwards. Work the foaming water in either glass beads or cross stitch using very light baby blue 3756. The colour chart key lists the shade codes for both.

2. When stitching the design use two strands of stranded cotton (floss) for the cross stitch, and one strand for the backstitch. Work the backstitch detail in black 310 around the body and fins, and use dark shell grey 451 around the lower part of the gills.

TO MAKE UP THE WALL HANGING
1. From the felt, with pinking shears, cut one rectangle, 34 x 43cm (13½ x 17in), and two 6.5 x 17cm (2½ x 6¾in) strips for the hanging loops. From the hessian (jute), cut one rectangle, 29 x 38cm (11½ x 15in), and two 3.5 x 17cm (1½ x 6¾in) strips for the hanging loops.

2. With a soft pencil, draw a border around the stitched design, measuring 1.5cm (⅝in) from the side and bottom stitched edges, and 3.5cm (1½in) from the top of the fish. Trim away excess Aida fabric along the pencilled line.

3. Place the embroidered fabric centrally over the hessian (jute) patch. Pin and tack (baste) in place, then run a row of machine stitches 1cm (½in) from the outer edges. Place the hessian (jute) patch centrally over the felt shape, and

repeat the process, stitching 1.5cm (⅝in) from the outer edges. Finish both patches with a frayed edging by teasing out the threads at the outer edges. The row of machine stitches prevents the fabric from fraying too far.

4. To make the hanging loops, lay each hessian strip centrally over each felt strip. Pin and tack (baste) in place, then make several rows of machine stitches down the centre of each strip. Make a frayed edging as above.

5. Fold the strips in half to form a loop, then pin, tack (baste) and stitch in place, along the top edge of the wall hanging. Finally, thread a stick or hanging rod through the loops.

SALMON

Salmon instinctively embark on a journey of thousands of miles to spawn in the waters where they hatched. Their journey is strenuous as they swim against the flow of the river, through rapids and leap waterfalls. 'Salmon ladders' are built to help them reach their breeding ground, where many die from exhaustion after spawning.

DMC

	801
	938
	3371
	677
	676
	729
	680
	732
	733
	500
	501
	502
	931
	932
	3752
	3753
	726
	725
	452
	451
	535
	3052
	3051
	3064
	3772
	632
	414
	318
	415
	762
	white
	310
	3756

or
Mill Hill
glass beads
Crystal 00161

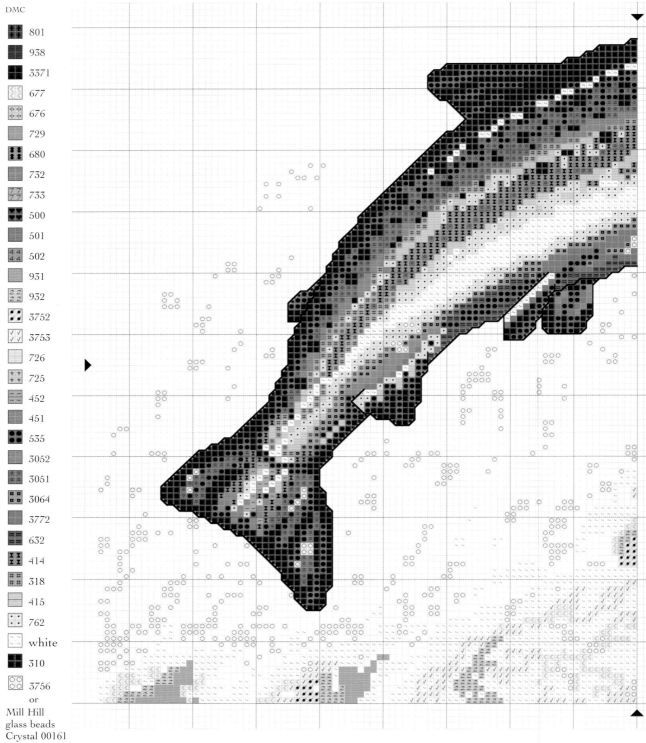

Estuary Flowers Clock

This charming clock features a simple estuary scene surrounded by bunches of purple and pink sea-pea flowers. The sea-pea is a relative of the fragrant sweet-pea and is found along coastal areas. The design is worked on a 22-count Hardanger fabric using cross stitch, three-quarter cross stitch and backstitch. The pretty floral motifs could be used on their own to decorate trinkets and other needlework projects.

FINISHED DESIGN SIZE
13 x 18cm (5 x 7in) approximately

WHAT YOU WILL NEED
- Antique white 22-count Hardanger (E1008), 33 x 38cm (13 x 15in)
- Mantle clock (available from Framecraft – see Stockists page 127)

DMC STRANDED COTTON (FLOSS)
1 SKEIN
Black 310; white; very dark violet 550; med violet 552; violet 553; dark plum 915; med plum 917; very light plum 3608; light plum 3609; baby pink 818; med yellow green 3347; hunter green 3346; dark hunter green 3345; very dark hunter green 895; very light tan 739; med brown 433; dark coffee brown 801; light antique blue 932; med antique blue 931; very light blue 827

1. Prepare your fabric for work, reading the Techniques section if necessary. Refer to the Stitch Guide pages 11–13 for the stitches.
2. Work the central estuary design and the clock face first, then the flowers and foliage around the edges, using two strands of stranded cotton (floss) for the cross stitch and one strand for the backstitch. Note: when the design is stitched there should be more fabric at the top than at the bottom (see arrow on chart).

3. Work the backstitch detail in very dark hunter green 895 for the flower stems and black 310 for the seagulls. Work the Roman numerals for the clock dial in long stitches, using two strands of black 310.
4. When you have completed the design, refer to the manufacturer's instructions for mounting the embroidery into the clock.

SEA-PEA
This pretty flower grows in large patches along the shingle beaches, banks and sand dunes in south-east Britain, Scandinavia, Germany, Japan, the Great Lakes and the north-west of America. It flowers in Britain in May and June and is pollinated by bumble bees. The seeds find their way into the sea, where they can remain floating and dormant for up to five years. In England, there was a famine in 1555, and the people of Suffolk survived by eating the seeds from these flowers, which grew in abundance along the coast.

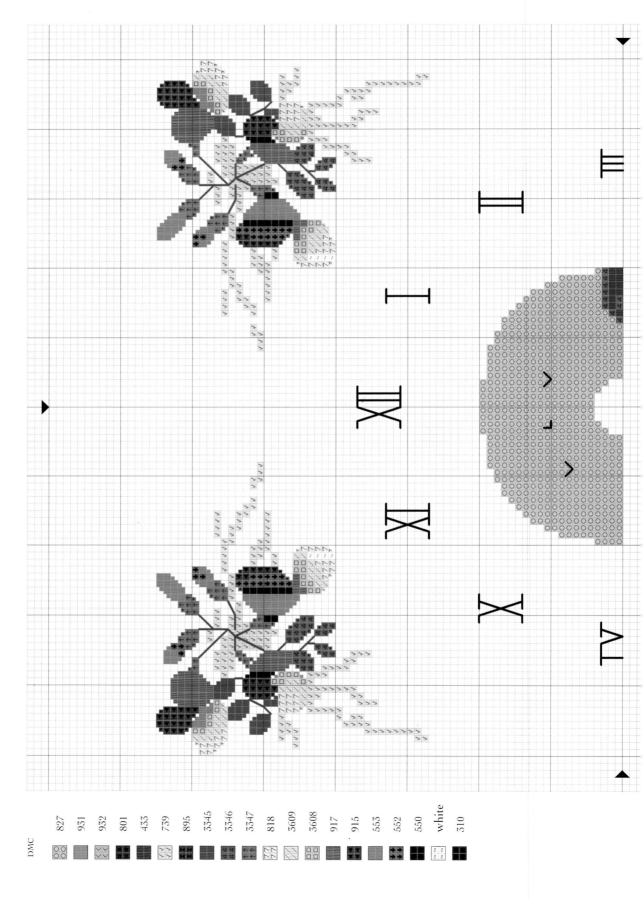

DMC	
827	
931	
932	
801	
433	
739	
895	
3345	
3346	
3347	
818	
3609	
3608	
917	
915	
553	
552	
550	
white	
310	

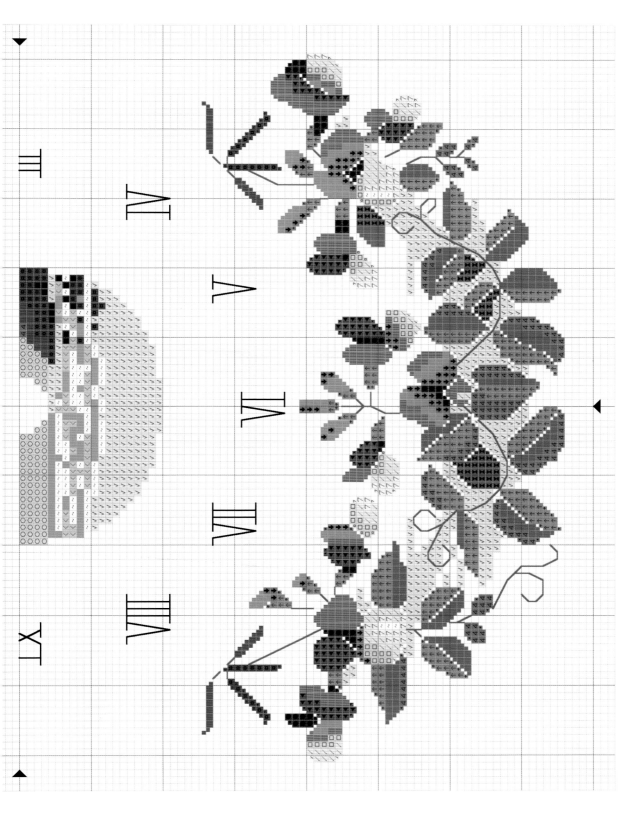

Cormorant Cushion and Picture

This beautiful design shows a tranquil scene along the estuary: a cormorant perched on a wooden post fans out its wings and a moored rowing boat reflects upon the rippling waters. The same design is used for a picture and a cushion but the cushion has a knotted rope border, echoing the muted background colours. Both items are worked on 14-count Aida with cross stitch, three-quarter cross stitch, backstitch and a tiny French knot.

Cormorant Cushion

FINISHED DESIGN SIZE
Design with border, 35.5cm (14in) square
approximately

WHAT YOU WILL NEED
- White 14-count Aida, 50cm (20in) square
- Cotton fabric for backing, 30 x 90cm
  (⅜yd x 36in) wide
- Thick furnishing braid, 1.7m (1⅞yd)
- Matching sewing thread
- Square cushion pad to fit

DMC STRANDED COTTON (FLOSS)
1 SKEIN

Black 310; white; dark pistachio green 890; dark emerald green 3818; very dark emerald green 909; dark emerald green 910; off-white 746; very light old gold 677; light old gold 676; med old gold 729; dark old gold 680; dark golden olive 830; very dark golden olive 829; dark coffee brown 938; black brown 3371; red copper 919; dark red copper 918; light beaver grey 648; med beaver grey 647; very dark beaver grey 645; very light grey green 928; light grey green 927; light grey green 926; dark grey green 3768; light drab brown 613; med drab brown 612; dark drab brown 611; dark coffee brown 801; very dark pistachio green 319; light tangerine 742; dark pistachio green 367; dark olive green 731; med olive green 733; med shell grey 452; light shell grey 453; med yellow 743; pale yellow 744; light pale yellow 745; light brown 434

1. Prepare your fabric for work, reading the Techniques section if necessary. Refer to the Stitch Guide pages 11–13 for how to work the stitches, working the design from the centre outwards. Work the rope border last.

2. When stitching the design use two strands of stranded cotton (floss) for the cross stitch. Work the backstitch using two strands of black 310 for the boat's mooring ropes. Use one strand of black 310 to outline the eye, beak, wing and tail feathers, and light brown 434 to work the rope border. Work a French knot using one strand of white for the eye highlight.

TO MAKE UP THE CUSHION

1. For the cushion front, cut away excess fabric to within 4cm (1¾in) of the finished embroidery, to allow for a 1.5cm (⅝in) seam allowance.

2. For the cushion backs, cut two pieces of cotton fabric 30 x 44cm (11¾ x 17¼in), then take each rectangle and hem one long edge.

3. Lay the embroidered fabric face upwards on a flat surface. With right sides facing down, lay the cushion backs over the front so that all raw edges match and the hemmed edges overlap at the centre. Pin, tack (baste) and machine stitch along the stitching line, through all layers of fabric. Neaten the raw edges, then turn the cover through to the right side.

4. To finish, hand stitch the furnishing braid around the edge of the cushion cover and insert a square cushion pad.

CORMORANT
Cormorants are found in both salt and fresh waters. They breed in close colonies consisting of hundreds or thousands of birds and build their nests of twigs and seaweed on cliff ledges, or even in tree tops. They swim low in the water with their heads held high and then effortlessly dive under the water in pursuit of fish. All four toes are webbed which helps them swim underwater. When they emerge from the water, they stand on a perch with wings outstretched, not to dry themselves but to aid their metabolism. The Chinese and Japanese train these birds from chicks, to dive and catch fish for them.

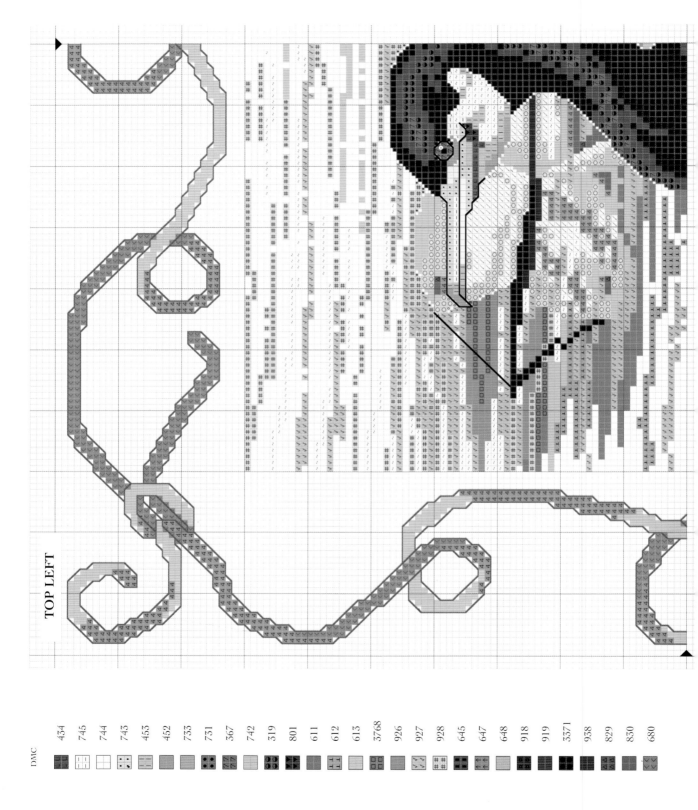

TOP LEFT

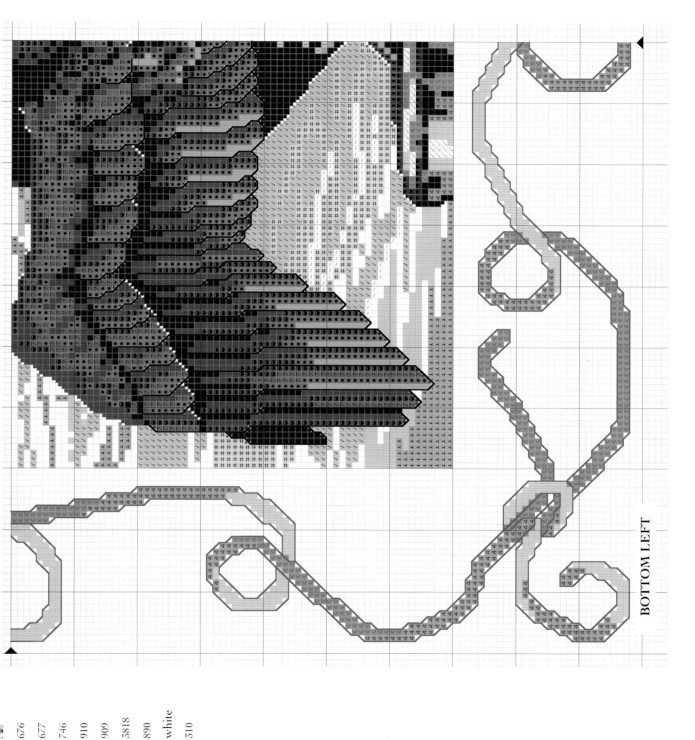

BOTTOM LEFT

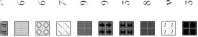

676 677 746 910 909 3818 890 white 310

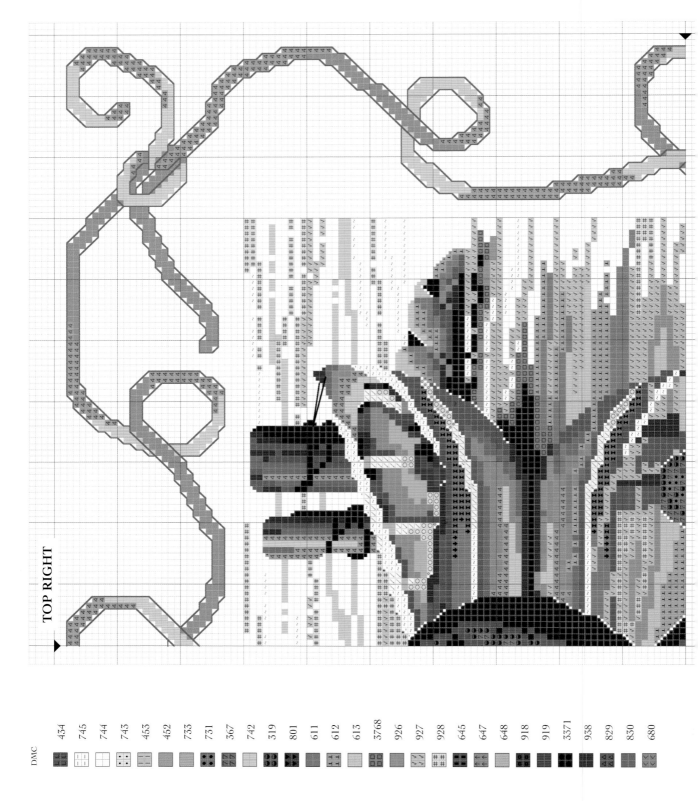

TOP RIGHT

DMC

| 434 | 745 | 744 | 743 | 453 | 452 | 733 | 731 | 367 | 742 | 319 | 801 | 611 | 612 | 613 | 3768 | 926 | 927 | 928 | 645 | 647 | 648 | 918 | 919 | 3371 | 938 | 829 | 830 | 680 |

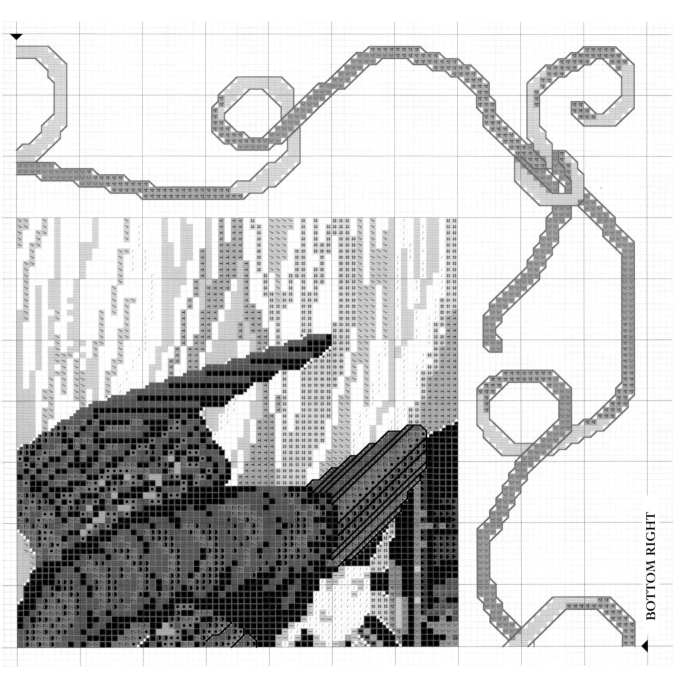

BOTTOM RIGHT

729 676 677 746 910 909 3818 890 white 310

Cormorant Picture

FINISHED DESIGN SIZE
Bird design (excluding rope border), 25.5cm (10in)
square approximately

WHAT YOU WILL NEED
• White 14-count Aida, 40.5cm (16in) square

DMC STRANDED COTTON (FLOSS)
Follow the thread list for the Cormorant Cushion on
page 73

1. Prepare your fabric for work, reading the
Techniques section if necessary. Refer to the
Stitch Guide pages 11–13 for how to work
the stitches, working the design from the centre
outwards.

2. Stitch the design following the charts on
pages 74–77, using two strands of stranded
cotton (floss) for the cross stitch. Work the
backstitch using two strands of stranded cotton
(floss) in black 310 for the boat's mooring ropes.
Use one strand of black 310 to outline the eye,
beak, wing and tail feathers. Work a French
knot using one strand of white for the
eye highlight.

3. Refer to Mounting and Framing page 10 for
how to complete your picture.

Brown Bears Picture

Brown bears live mainly on carrion, insects, honey and fruits; they also can't resist fish, as this design shows. The design uses just cross stitch, making it an ideal project to experiment with different threads and fabrics. It is worked on a 28-count evenweave fabric with each cross stitch worked over two threads, but it would be the same size if worked on a 14-count Aida. It is not necessary to stitch the sky if using a pale blue fabric.

FINISHED DESIGN SIZE
29 x 37cm (11½ x 14½in) approximately

WHAT YOU WILL NEED
• Ice blue 28-count Annabelle (E3240), 43 x 50cm (17 x 20in)

DMC STRANDED COTTON (FLOSS)
1 SKEIN
Light tan 437; tan 436; very light brown 435; light brown 434; med brown 433; dark coffee brown 801; dark coffee brown 938; pewter grey 317; dark pewter grey 413; very dark pewter grey 3799; very light antique blue 3753; very light antique blue 3752; light antique blue 932; med antique blue 931; dark antique blue 930; very dark antique blue 3750; very light shell pink 224; light coral 352; black avocado green 934; med avocado green 937; avocado green 469; light avocado green 470; light beige grey 822; med beige grey 644; dark beige grey 642; very dark beige grey 3790; very dark brown grey 3021; dark brown grey 3787; med brown grey 3022; med mustard 370; mustard 371; light mustard 372; med pistachio green 320; dark pistachio green 367; very dark pistachio green 319; dark pistachio green 890
2 SKEINS
Black 310; white; black brown 3371

1. Prepare your fabric for work, reading the Techniques section if necessary. Refer to the Stitch Guide pages 11–13 for how to work the stitches, working the design from the centre outwards.

2. When stitching the design use two strands of stranded cotton (floss) for the cross stitch, worked over two threads of evenweave fabric. If you are stitching on white evenweave instead of the blue we have used, you could stitch the sky area using light baby blue 3325.

3. Refer to Mounting and Framing page 10 for how to complete your picture.

BROWN BEARS

Brown bears are found in Europe, Asia and North America, and increase in size and weight the further north they get. These powerful creatures earned enormous respect from the indigenous people of North America and hold a significant place in their culture and mythology. The ancient practice of 'dancing' bears features in Indian and Turkish folklore and is still common in Greece today. Bears were owned by gypsies who captured cubs and trained them by placing hot trays under their feet and playing music at the same time. The bear learned to associate music with pain, and so 'danced' when they heard music.

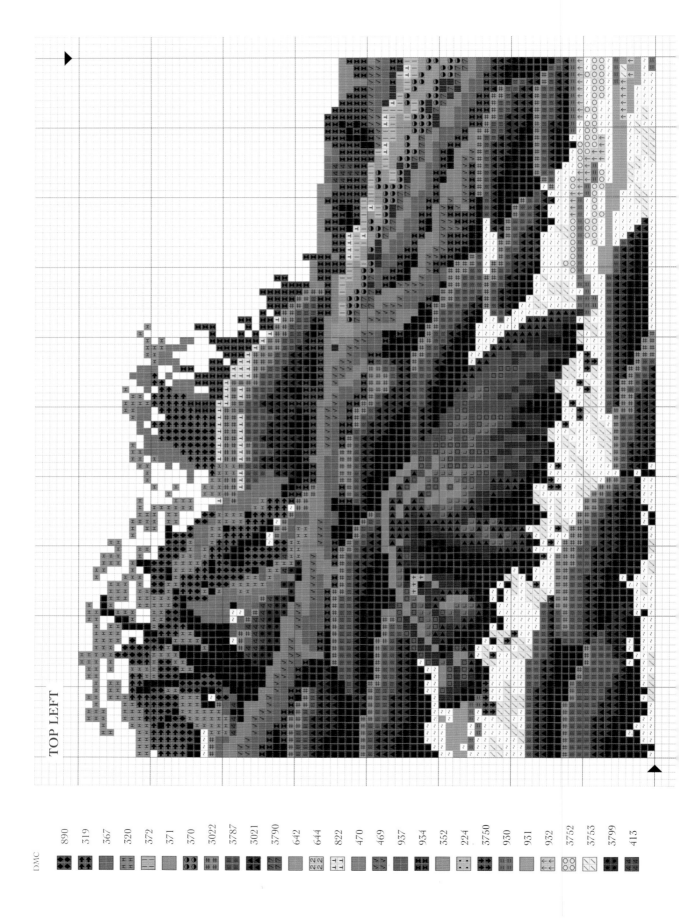

TOP LEFT

DMC 890 319 367 320 372 371 370 3022 3787 3021 3790 642 644 822 470 469 937 934 352 224 3750 930 951 932 3752 3753 3799 413

BOTTOM LEFT

317 3371 958 801 433 434 435 436 437 white 310

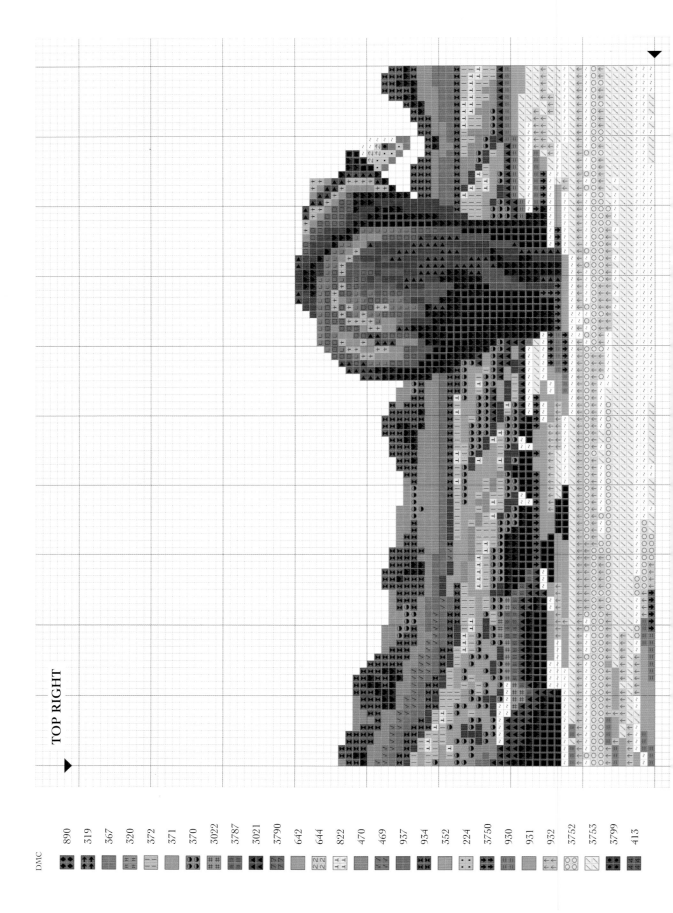

TOP RIGHT

DMC																													
890	319	367	320	372	371	370	3022	3787	3021	3790	642	644	822	470	469	957	954	352	224	3750	930	951	952	3752	3753	3799	413

BOTTOM RIGHT

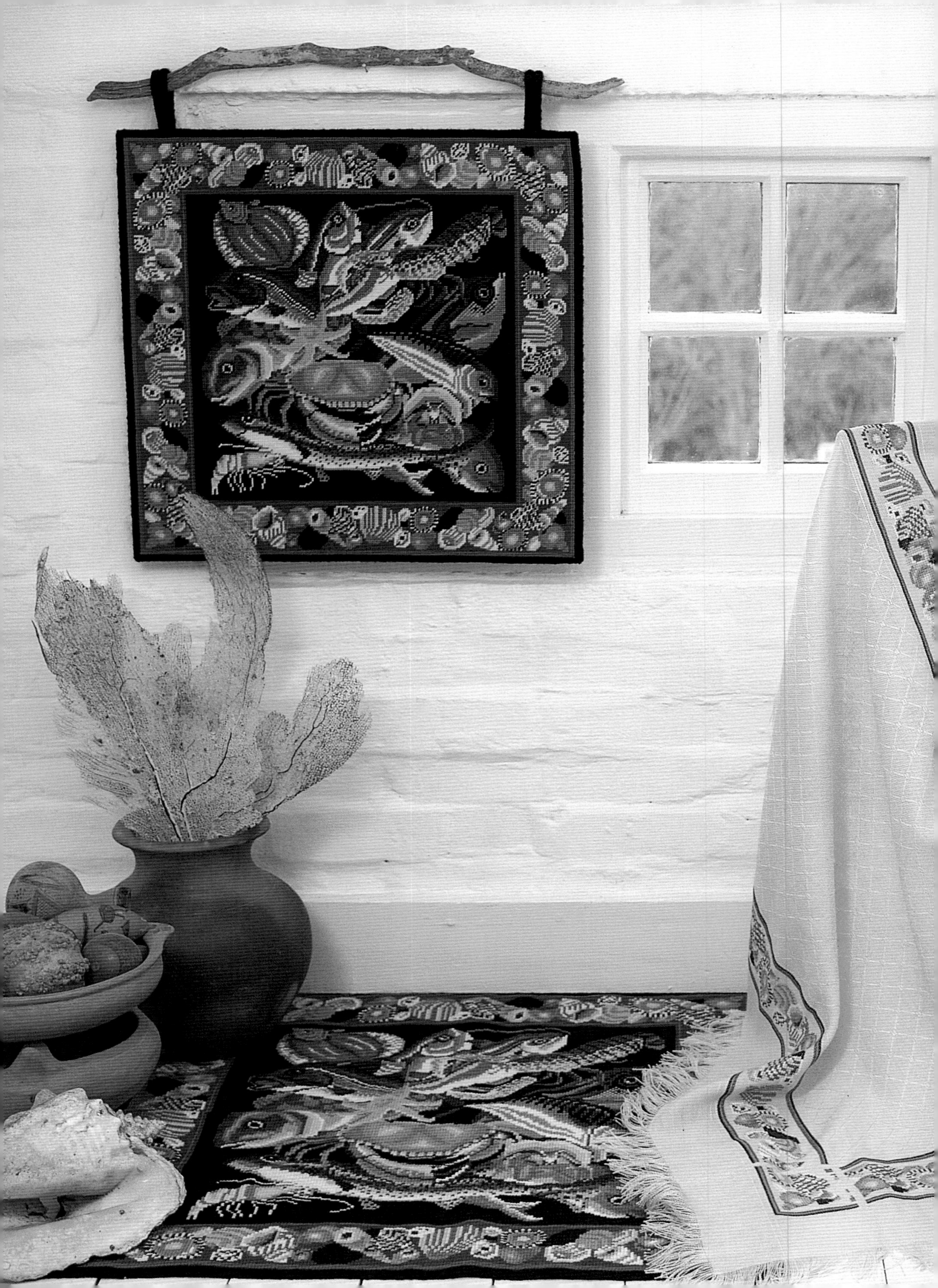

All At Sea

The glory of the sea and the mysteries held within its underwater world have been captured in this collection of stunning designs beginning with a rock-pool collage of shells and fishes decorating a fabulous rug, a wall hanging and a throw (all pictured here).

People have always been fascinated with the sea and many brave sailors lost their lives on boats like the one featured on the Clipper Ship Fire-screen. Away from the high seas, the rocky reefs and shores provide a home to many creatures, while the sandy beaches, rocks and cliffs of the surrounding coastline host an abundance of wild flowers. A delightful collection of sewing accessories and gifts are worked with delicate designs of yellow-horned poppies, rock sea-spurry and bindweed flowers.

Wildlife at sea varies from the smallest known organisms to the largest of whales and everything else in between. Our beautiful dolphin picture and footstool show dolphins at play, surrounded by a decorative border of tropical fishes and coral reefs. The sea creature theme is carried on to a child's bedroom accessories using simple designs of tiny boats and fishes, buckets and spades, starfish and sea-horses, worked on 14-count Aida and 6-count Zweibinca to create a colourful picture, rug, cushions and soft toys.

The frozen polar regions are the coldest places on earth, and are home to polar bears and penguins, providing inspiration for two stunning designs. So whichever project you choose to stitch, it will be a reminder of the sea, and the mysteries within it.

Rock-Pool Collage

This stunning design has a central panel of fish and rock-pool creatures and an intricate shell border. The rug and wall hanging use tapestry wool (yarn) for crabs, starfish, lobsters, prawns, mackerel, cod and plaice. The throw uses cottons in a shell border. The colour key lists cottons and wools so you can work in either.

Rock-Pool Shells Throw

FINISHED DESIGN SIZE
72 x 104cm (28¼ x 41in) approximately

WHAT YOU WILL NEED
• Cream evenweave Abbey Cloth (E7573),
  1.1m x 145cm (1¼yd x 57in) wide
• Matching sewing thread

DMC STRANDED COTTON (FLOSS)
1 SKEIN
Med old gold 729; dark old gold 680; very light orange spice 3825; med orange spice 721; dark orange spice 720; light steel grey 318; very light pistachio green 369; light pistachio green 368; dark pistachio green 367; navy blue 336; dark navy blue 823; topaz 725; very dark topaz 781; very dark topaz 780; light beige brown 841

2 SKEINS
White; very light old gold 677; light old gold 676; light orange spice 722; very dark mahogany 300; dark coffee brown 938; pearl grey 415; med topaz 783; dark topaz 782; very light beige brown 842

3 SKEINS
Red copper 919; very dark old gold 3829; off-white 746

4 SKEINS
Black 310

1. Abbey cloth has tramlines running through it creating a panel with a trellis design, surrounded by gridlines which form a border. This border will be stitched with the shell design from the main charts overleaf. You will need a rectangle of fabric 1.1m x 145cm (1¼yd x 57in), with the trellis panel at the centre. Run several rows of machine stitches 8cm (3¼in) from the outer edges to create the fringing later.

2. When stitching the design use three strands of stranded cotton (floss) for the cross stitch and work over two threads.

3. Begin stitching the outer border lines, by working one row of cross stitch in black 310, one row in very dark old gold 3829 and one row in red copper 919. Then count the width of the shell border and stitch the inner border lines, using the colours in reverse order.

4. Now work the shells themselves between these border gridlines, omitting the background colour red copper 919. To make the shell design fit along each border edge of the throw, work the design starting at each left corner of the throw, then follow the chart to stitch one complete edge of the shell design. Continue repeating the shell design to fit along the length of the gridlines on the throw.

5. To finish, tease out the threads at the outer edges to make a fringe. The machine stitches will prevent the fabric from fraying too far.

Rock-Pool Wall Hanging

FINISHED DESIGN SIZE
56cm (22in) square approximately

WHAT YOU WILL NEED
- White 10-count Interlock canvas (E604A), 68cm (27in) square
- Large tapestry frame (optional)
- Large tapestry needle
- Thimble
- Hanging rod or stick, 66cm (26in) long
- Flat braid, 40cm (16in)
- Sewing thread

DMC TAPESTRY WOOL (YARN), 8m SKEINS
1 SKEIN
Dark old gold 7421; med orange spice 7214; very dark mahogany 7458; med brown 7479; light brown 7845; pewter grey 7705; dark pewter grey 7713; very light pistachio green 7382; light pistachio green 7384; dark pistachio green 7320; navy blue 7336; dark navy blue 7299; topaz 7971; med topaz 7506; dark topaz 7783; very dark topaz 7767; very dark topaz 7780; light beige brown 7519; very light mahogany 7175; light mahogany 7444; med mahogany 7457; med olive green 7583; olive green 7364; fern green 7376; dark fern green 7396; dark peacock blue 7813; very dark peacock blue 7650; pale yellow 7727; med yellow 7725; light tangerine 7050; dark beige grey 7416; very dark beige grey 7415; dark beige grey 7413
2 SKEINS
Very light old gold 7579; med old gold 7494; very light orange spice 7173; light orange spice 7009; dark orange spice 7875; light steel grey 7282; very light beige brown 7520
3 SKEINS
White, very dark old gold 7477; ecru; light old gold 7503; dark coffee brown 7489; pearl grey 7292
7 SKEINS
Red copper 7303
DMC TAPESTRY WOOL (YARN), 38m SKEINS
4 SKEINS
Black 7310

1. Prepare your canvas for work, reading the Techniques section if necessary. Rug canvas tends to stretch and loose its shape easily. To prevent this, and to make working easier, mount the work on to a large tapestry frame. Refer to Stitch Guide pages 11–13 for the stitches.

2. Following the charts overleaf, work from the centre outwards, starting with the central rock-pool panel, then adding the border. Use a large tapestry needle and a thimble to protect your fingers. Use one strand of tapestry wool (yarn) throughout for the half cross stitch.

3. When the design is completed, trim away excess canvas to within 5cm (2in) of the stitches. Fold the canvas turnings to the back of the wall hanging, leaving one hole showing and one thread running across the top of the fold. Stitch the turnings in place.

4. Overcast the edges, following step 4 page 94 for the rock-pool rug, using two strands of wool (yarn) in the needle and working one stitch in each hole to cover the canvas completely.

5. Cut two 20cm (8in) strips of flat braid. Fold the strips in half to form a loop, then hand stitch them at the back of the wall hanging, either end of the top edge. Finally, thread a hanging rod through the loops and hang in place.

ROCK-POOLS

If you look really hard into a rock-pool it's amazing what a wide range of creatures you can find. Most pools usually provide a home for small fish, tiny crabs and sea anemones but if you are really lucky you may see a starfish or even prawns, which are difficult to spot because they are transparent. Although we all love to collect shells as we walk along the water's edge, they shouldn't really be removed from the beach. Discarded shells are used as homes by other creatures, such as hermit crabs who favour the shells of winkles and whelks. Other shells are ground up by the pounding waves and are turned into shingle and, eventually, into sand.

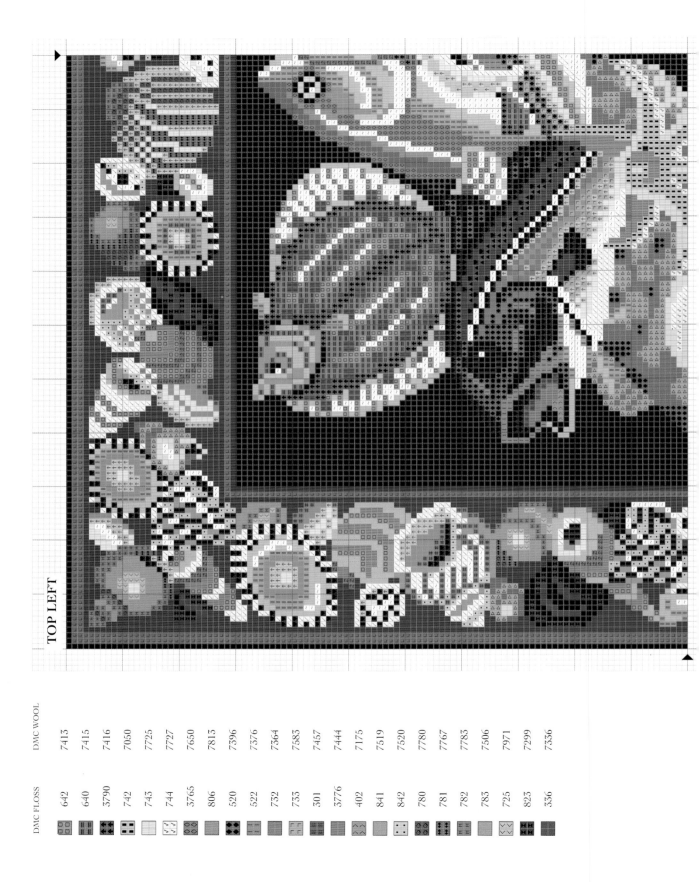

TOP LEFT

DMC WOOL	DMC FLOSS
7413	642
7415	640
7416	3790
7050	742
7725	743
7727	744
7650	3765
7813	806
7396	520
7376	522
7364	732
7585	733
7457	301
7444	3776
7175	402
7519	841
7520	842
7780	780
7767	781
7783	782
7506	783
7971	725
7299	823
7336	336

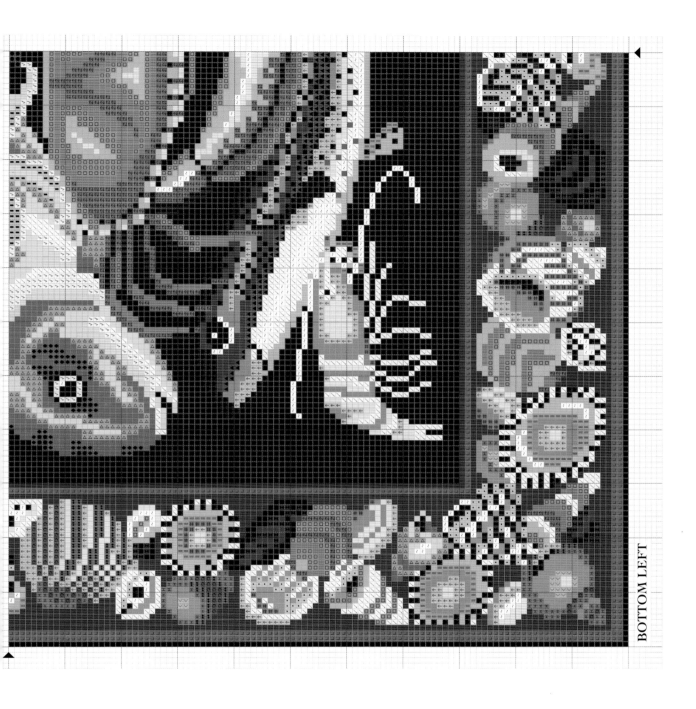

BOTTOM LEFT

367	368	369	415	317	318	415	434	433	938	300	720	721	722	3825	680	729	676	677	746	3829	919	white	310
7320	7384	7382	7713	7705	7282	7292	7845	7479	7489	7458	7875	7214	7009	7173	7421	7494	7503	7579	ecru	7477	7303	white	7310

TOP RIGHT

DMC WOOL	DMC FLOSS
7413	642
7415	640
7416	3790
7050	742
7725	743
7727	744
7650	3765
7813	806
7396	520
7376	522
7364	732
7583	733
7457	301
7444	3776
7175	402
7519	841
7520	842
7780	780
7767	781
7783	782
7506	783
7971	725
7299	823
7336	336

ALL AT SEA

BOTTOM RIGHT

DMC FLOSS	DMC WOOL	
367	7320	
368	7384	
369	7382	
413	7713	
317	7705	
318	7282	
415	7292	
434	7845	
433	7479	
938	7489	
300	7458	
720	7875	
721	7214	
722	7009	
3825	7173	
680	7421	
729	7494	
676	7503	
677	7579	
746	ecru	
3829	7477	
919	7303	
white	white	
310	7310	

Rock-Pool Rug

FINISHED DESIGN SIZE

76cm (30in) square approximately (including shell border)

WHAT YOU WILL NEED

- Ecru 7-count Sudan canvas (E699), 120cm (48in) square
- Large tapestry frame (optional)
- Large tapestry needle
- Thimble

DMC TAPESTRY WOOL (YARN), 8m SKEINS
1 SKEIN

Med brown 7479; light brown 7845; very light pistachio green 7382; navy blue 7336; topaz 7971; very light mahogany 7175; light mahogany 7444; med mahogany 7457; med olive green 7583; olive green 7364; fern green 7376; dark peacock blue 7813; pale yellow 7727; med yellow 7725; light tangerine 7050

2 SKEINS

Dark old gold 7421; pewter grey 7705; dark pewter grey 7713; light pistachio green 7384; dark pistachio green 7320; med topaz 7506; dark topaz 7783; very dark topaz 7767; very dark topaz 7780; light beige brown 7519; dark fern green 7396; very dark peacock blue 7650; dark beige grey 7416; very dark beige grey 7415; dark beige grey 7413

3 SKEINS

Med old gold 7494; very light orange spice 7173; light orange spice 7009; med orange spice 7214; very dark mahogany 7458; light steel grey 7282; dark navy blue 7299; very light beige brown 7520

4 SKEINS

Dark orange spice 7875

5 SKEINS

White; very light old gold 7579; light old gold 7503; dark coffee brown 7489; pearl grey 7292

7 SKEINS

Very dark old gold 7477; ecru

13 SKEINS

Red copper 7303

DMC TAPESTRY WOOL (YARN), 38m SKEINS
7 SKEINS

Black 7310

---

1. Prepare your canvas for work, reading the Techniques section if necessary. Rug canvas tends to stretch and loose its shape easily. To prevent this, and to make working easier, it is best to mount the work on to a large tapestry frame.

2. The design is worked in cross stitch with one strand of tapestry wool (yarn). Work from the centre outwards, starting with the central rock-pool panel, then adding the border (see photograph on page 86). Use a large tapestry needle and a thimble to protect your fingers.

3. When the design is completed, trim away excess canvas to within 10cm (4in) of the stitches. Fold the canvas turnings to the back of the rug, leaving one hole showing and one thread running across the top of the fold. Stitch the turnings in place.

4. Finish the rug by adding an overcast edging. To do this, use two strands of black 7310, secure the thread at the back of the canvas, insert the needle into the hole nearest the cross stitches and pull to the front of the canvas. The overcast thread should share a hole with the last stitch of the cross stitch design. Take the needle to the back of the canvas and work the next stitch in the same way (fig 17). Work two or three stitches in each hole to cover the canvas completely.

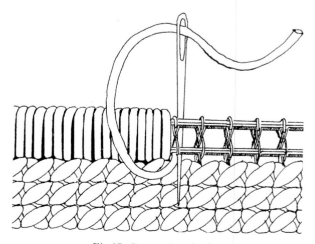

Fig 17 Overcasting the edge

Playful Dolphins

Of all the creatures in the sea, dolphins are a popular favourite. This design of dolphins at play, surrounded by a border of tropical fish and coral reef, is worked in cross stitch, three-quarter cross stitch and backstitch, against a blue background. The whole design, mounted onto a square footstool, is worked on 14-count Aida. Alternatively, you could just work the central panel on 28-count evenweave fabric for the beautiful dolphin picture.

Dolphin Footstool

FINISHED DESIGN SIZE
32cm (12½in) diameter approximately

WHAT YOU WILL NEED
• Cadet blue 14-count Aida, 50cm (20in) square
• Footstool 36cm (14in) square (available from MacGregor Designs – see Stockists page 127)

DMC STRANDED COTTON (FLOSS)
1 SKEIN
Dolphins: Black 310; white; dark turquoise 3808; very dark pewter grey 3799; dark pewter grey 413; pewter grey 317; dark steel grey 414; light steel grey 318; pearl grey 415; very light pearl grey 762; very dark antique blue 3750; dark antique blue 930; very light blue 827; light blue 813
2 SKEINS
Very light blue 828

1 SKEIN
Border: Black 310; white; light turquoise 598; turquoise 597; dark turquoise 3808; light beige grey 822; med beige grey 644; dark beige grey 642; dark beige grey 3790; light mustard 372; mustard 371; med mustard 370; very dark drab brown 610; med blue violet 340; pale yellow 744; med topaz 783; dark lemon 444; lemon 307; light lemon 445; light peacock blue 3766; peacock blue 807; dark peacock blue 806; light steel grey 318; pearl grey 415; very light pearl grey 762; dark blue 825; very light baby blue 775; very light blue 827
3 SKEINS
Very light turquoise 3811

1. Prepare your fabric for work, reading the Techniques section if necessary. Refer to the Stitch Guide pages 11–13 for the stitches, working the design from the centre outwards.
2. When stitching the design use two strands of stranded cotton (floss) for the cross stitch and one strand for the backstitch. Work the backstitch detail in very dark pewter grey 3799 to outline the dolphins, and black 310 to outline the fish in the border.
3. To mount the embroidery in the footstool, refer to the manufacturer's instructions.

Above: A detail of the fabulous dolphin picture, showing the intricate stitching and marine thread colours

BOTTLE-NOSED DOLPHIN

Bottle-nosed dolphins are the largest of the dolphins and are distinguished by their short, well-defined snout. These clever, swift creatures are not fish but mammals and have complicated brains which are the most comparable to our own. Commonly found in the Atlantic, they survive on sharks, shrimps, rays and cuttlefish, and communicate with each other by high-pitched whistles and grunts. Today, these beautiful creatures are widely kept in captivity and are the most common performers in many of the sea worlds. Ancient Mediterranean cultures believed that dolphins represented the vital power of the sea and killing a dolphin was punishable by death.

Dolphin Picture

FINISHED DESIGN SIZE
20.5cm (8in) diameter approximately

WHAT YOU WILL NEED
• Ice blue 28-count evenweave Annabel (E3240),
38cm (15in) square

DMC STRANDED COTTON (FLOSS)
Use the thread list for the Dolphin Footstool on page
96, using 1 skein of each colour. If you wish to leave the
sky unstitched, as we have done, omit 2 skeins of very
light blue 828

1. Prepare your fabric for work, reading the Techniques section if necessary. Refer to the Stitch Guide pages 11–13 for the stitches, working the design from the centre outwards.
2. Using the charts overleaf, work the dolphins and the sea, then the first row only of the inner border to frame the design, using two strands of stranded cotton (floss) for the cross stitch and one strand for the backstitch, over two threads of evenweave fabric. Work the back-stitch detail in very dark pewter grey 3799 to outline the dolphins.
3. Refer to Mounting and Framing page 10 for how to complete your picture.

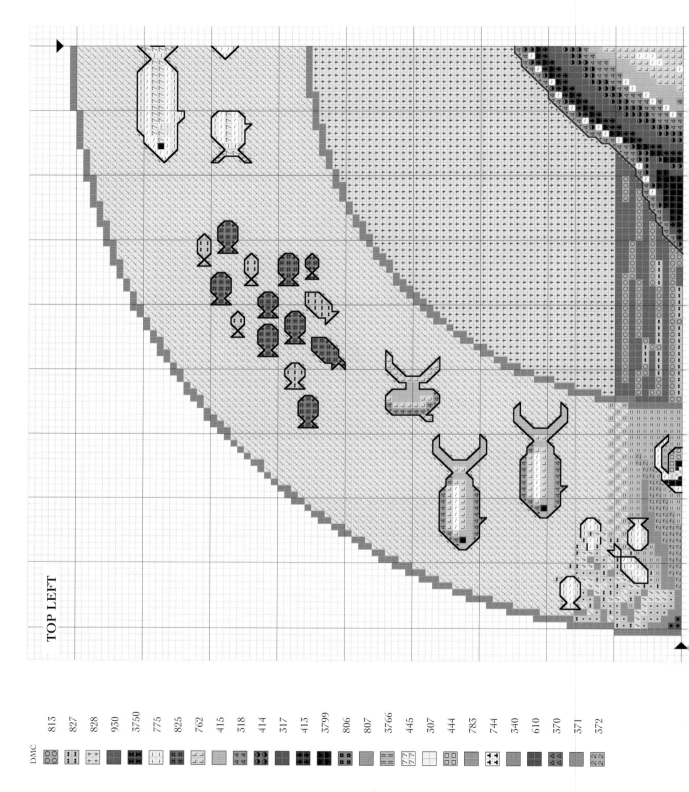

TOP LEFT

DMC

813 827 828 930 3750 775 825 762 415 318 414 317 413 3799 806 807 3766 445 307 444 783 744 340 610 370 371 372

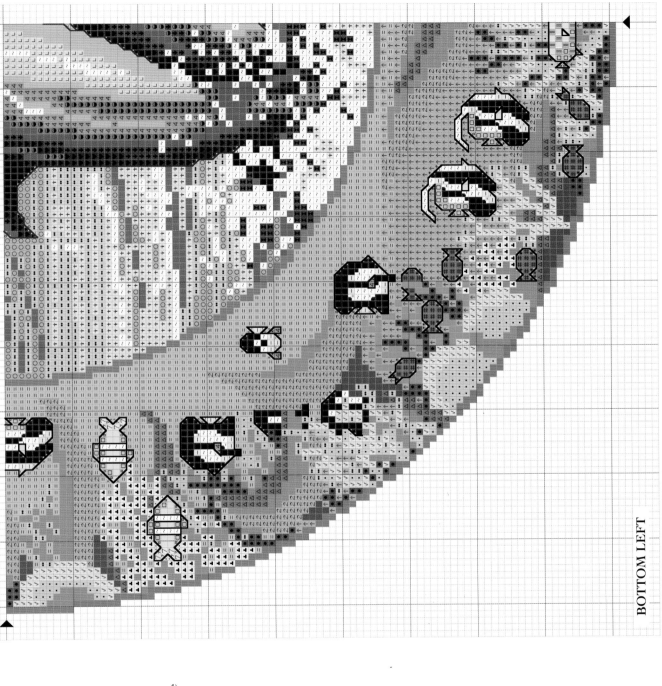

BOTTOM LEFT

3790 642 644 822 3808 597 598 3811 white 310

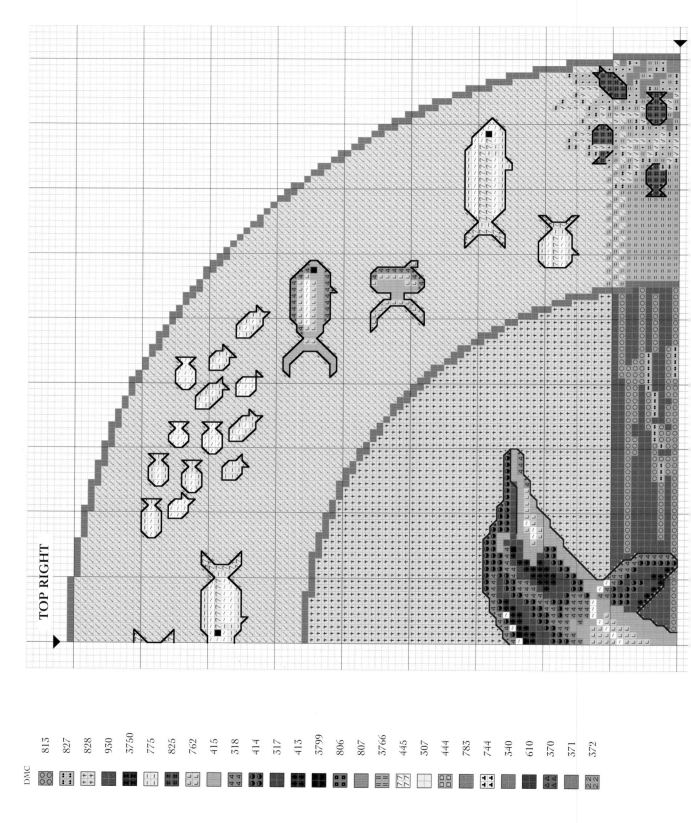

TOP RIGHT

DMC	813	827	828	930	3750	775	825	762	415	318	414	517	413	3799	806	807	3766	445	307	444	783	744	340	610	370	371	372

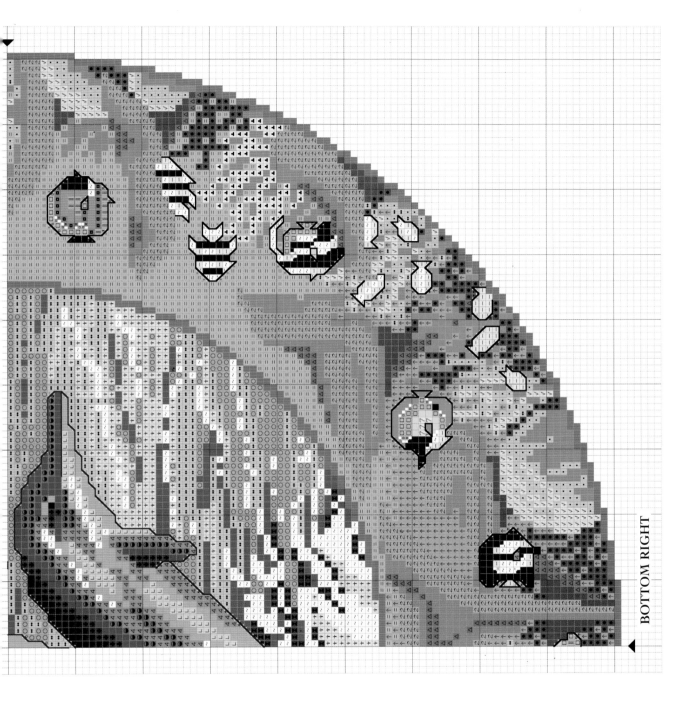

BOTTOM RIGHT

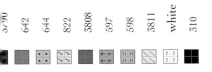

Clipper Ship Fire-Screen

This fire-screen shows a full-rigger in all its glory, sailing through stormy seas. Creamy-white sails are set against a grey sky, dark blue sea and frothy waves. The design is worked in half cross stitch using tapestry wool (yarn) but the colour key gives the shade codes for both tapestry wool and stranded cotton (floss) so the design can be worked using either.

FINISHED DESIGN SIZE
38 x 50cm (15 x 20in) approximately

WHAT YOU WILL NEED
- White 10-count single thread interlock canvas (E604A), 56 x 68cm (22 x 27in)
- Fire-screen for embroidery available from Market Square (see Stockists page 127)

DMC TAPESTRY WOOL (YARN)
1 SKEIN
Black 7310; light hazelnut brown 7494; med hazelnut brown 7513; dark hazelnut brown 7514; very dark hazelnut brown 7488; light old gold 7503; dark old gold 7421; black brown 7535; dark coffee brown 7938; very dark mahogany 7458; dark mahogany 7700; very dark antique blue 7590; med antique blue 7306; light antique blue 7304; very light antique blue 7802; very light antique blue 7302; light blue green 7399; light blue green 7952; med blue green 7598; very light baby blue 7800; light baby blue 7799; baby blue 7798; med flesh 7121; flesh 7191; light brown grey 7282; med brown grey 7273; dark brown grey 7275; light antique violet 7790; med antique violet 7264

2 SKEINS
Ecru; very light tan 7746; dark antique blue 7297; very light brown grey 7280

4 SKEINS
White

13 SKEINS
Dark airforce blue 7034

1. Prepare your canvas for work, reading the Techniques section if necessary. Canvas tends to stretch and loose its shape easily. To prevent this, and to make working easier, mount the work on to a large embroidery frame.

2. Work the design from the centre outwards, using a large tapestry needle and a thimble to protect your fingers. Use one strand of tapestry wool (yarn) throughout for the half cross stitch.

3. When the main design is complete, stitch the outer border by working twenty-two rows of half cross stitch all round using dark airforce blue 7034.

4. Mount the embroidery into the fire-screen following the manufacturer's instructions.

CLIPPER SHIPS
The growth of trade in the early 1800s led to the need for faster ships. American ship-builders developed the clipper ship which was able to cross the seas at record speeds, trading in exotic spices, sugar, textiles, tobacco, and opium. British tea-clippers like the *Cutty Sark* could bring cargoes of tea from China to London in 100 days.

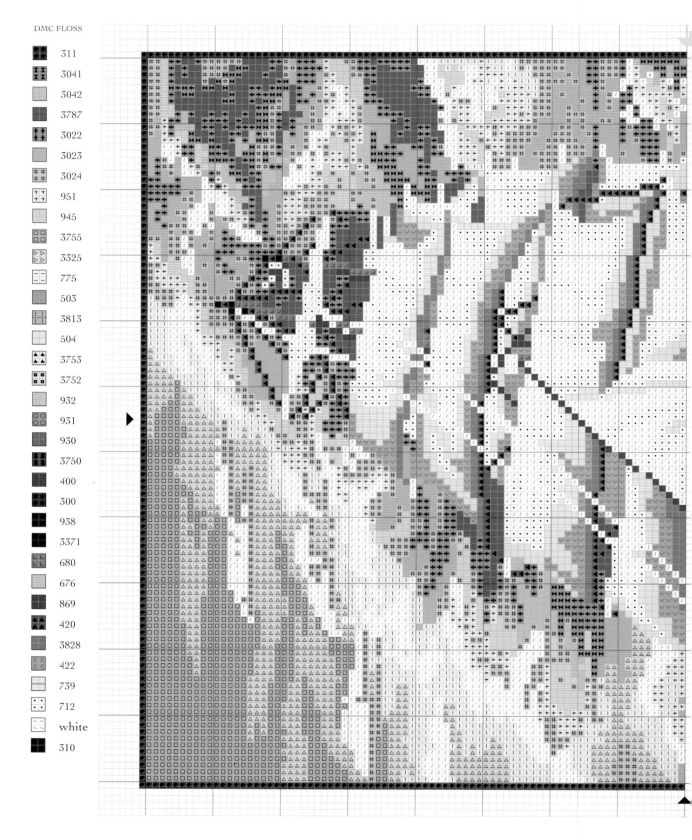

DMC FLOSS

311
3041
3042
3787
3022
3023
3024
951
945
3755
3325
775
503
3813
504
3753
3752
932
931
930
3750
400
300
938
3371
680
676
869
420
3828
422
739
712
white
310

DMC WOOL

	7034
	7264
	7790
	7275
	7273
	7282
	7280
	7191
	7121
	7798
	7799
	7800
	7598
	7952
	7399
	7302
	7802
	7304
	7306
	7297
	7590
	7700
	7458
	7938
	7535
	7421
	7503
	7488
	7514
	7513
	7494
	7746
	ecru
	white
	7310

Seashore Flowers

An abundance of flowers can be found along coastal paths, cliff tops and coastlines. Bindweed, sea-spurry, and yellow-horned poppies have been worked into pretty cross stitch designs to decorate gifts and simple sewing accessories. The designs are worked on 14-count Aida in a variety of colours. Small brass beads, buttons, ribbon and gingham binding are used to add the finishing touches to a glasses case, needlecase, herb sachet, pincushion and heart garland.

Sea-Spurry Pot-Pourri Sachet

FINISHED DESIGN SIZE
3.5cm (1½in) square approximately

WHAT YOU WILL NEED
- Cream damask 14-count Aida, the amount needed depends on the size of your sachet, our sachet is 8 x 13cm (3¼ x 5in)
- Decorative bias binding 20cm (¼yd), enough to bind the top edge of the sachet
- Satin ribbon, enough for a bow
- Matching sewing thread
- Pot-pourri for filling

DMC STRANDED COTTON (FLOSS)
1 SKEIN
Light topaz 726; very light avocado green 471; light avocado green 470; avocado green 469; med rose 899; rose 335

1. Prepare your fabric for work, reading the Techniques section if necessary. Refer to the Stitch Guide pages 11–13 for how to work the stitches, working the design from the centre outwards.

2. Stitch the sea-spurry design following the chart on page 110, using two strands of stranded cotton (floss) for the cross stitch and one strand for the backstitch. Work the backstitch detail in light avocado green 470 for the flower stems. If you wish, you could add a border around the whole design consisting of a double row of cross stitches worked on alternate blocks. Use stranded cotton (floss) light topaz 726 for the outer border and med rose 899 for the inner border.

TO MAKE UP THE SACHET
1. Once the design has been stitched, cut the embroidery to the size you want your sachet to be, adding 6mm (¼in) for seam allowances all the way round. Cut a piece of Aida fabric to the same size for the backing. With right sides facing, stitch the front and back pieces together along three sides leaving the top edge open.
2. Turn the sachet right sides out and finish the top edge with decorative bias binding (see making up step 3 page 108 as for the glasses case). Fill the sachet with pot-pourri and tie with a satin ribbon bow.

Sea Spurry Needlecase

FINISHED DESIGN SIZE
3.5cm (1½in) square approximately

WHAT YOU WILL NEED
- Lemon 14-count Aida, 23cm (9in) square
- Cream felt, 20cm (8in) square
- Decorative bias binding, 70cm (¾yd)
- Matching sewing thread
- Small domed button

DMC STRANDED COTTON (FLOSS)
1 SKEIN
Light topaz 726; very light avocado green 471; light avocado green 470; avocado green 469; med rose 899; rose 335

1. Prepare your fabric for work, reading the Techniques section if necessary. Refer to the Stitch Guide pages 11–13 for how to work the stitches, working the design from the centre outwards.

2. When stitching the sea-spurry design (refer to the chart, page 110) use two strands of stranded cotton (floss) for the cross stitch and one strand for the backstitch. Work the backstitch detail in light avocado green 470 for the flower stems. If you wish, you could add a border consisting of a double row of cross stitches, worked on alternate blocks. Use light topaz 726 for the outer border and med rose 899 for the inner border.

3. When the embroidery is complete, press carefully, then use a soft pencil to draw a rectangle all around the design, measuring 8 x 16cm (3¼ x 6½in), placing the stitching at one end. Cut away the excess fabric along these pencilled lines.

TO MAKE UP THE NEEDLECASE

1. Cut two pieces of felt for the inside 'pages' of the needlecase, measuring 6 x 14cm (2¼ x 5½in).

2. Bind all four edges of the Aida shape with bias binding. To make and attach the binding, follow making up step 3 for the yellow-horned poppy glasses case (below left).

3. Fold the Aida shape in half, so that both short edges meet, then tack (baste) a row of stitches along the fold line, to mark the centre. Lay the Aida shape right side down on a flat surface and place both felt shapes centrally over the Aida shape. Pin all three layers together, then machine stitch along the tacked (basted) centre line. Remove the pins.

4. Stitch a button to one short edge and make a thread loop at the other short edge, to keep the needlecase closed.

Yellow-Horned Poppy Glasses Case

FINISHED DESIGN SIZE
6 x 15cm (2¼ x 6in) approximately

WHAT YOU WILL NEED
- Cream 14-count Aida, 23 x 33cm (9 x 13in)
- Felt for lining, 25cm (10in) square
- Gingham fabric for backing and bias binding, 20cm x 90cm (¼yd x 36in) wide
- Matching sewing thread

DMC STRANDED COTTON (FLOSS)
1 SKEIN
Light pale yellow 745; very light topaz 727; light topaz 726; topaz 725; light pumpkin 970; med pistachio green 320; dark pistachio green 367; very dark pistachio green 319; very light avocado green 471

1. Prepare your fabric for work, reading the Techniques section if necessary. Refer to the Stitch Guide pages 11–13 for the stitches, working the design from the centre outwards.

2. When stitching the poppy design (see chart page 110) use two strands of stranded cotton (floss) for the cross stitch and one strand for the backstitch. Work the backstitch detail in very light avocado green 471 for the flowering grass stems, use topaz 725 around the flower petals and work the stems and flower centres in very dark pistachio green 319.

3. When the embroidery is complete, press, then use a soft pencil to draw a rectangle all around the design, measuring 12 x 20cm (4¾ x 8in). Cut away excess fabric along these lines.

TO MAKE UP THE GLASSES CASE

1. Cut two pieces of felt for the lining and one piece of gingham for the backing, to the same size as the embroidery.

2. Lay the two felt shapes side by side on a flat surface and, with right sides facing up, place the Aida and gingham fabric shapes on top of each felt shape. Tack (baste) both layers together to form the front and back pieces of the case then sew bias binding to the top short edge of each shape. To make the bias binding see page 10. Alternatively, you could use a ready-made binding (in which case you would need to buy less gingham fabric).

3. To attach the bias binding, open out the folded edges, lay the binding along the edge to be bound so that right sides are facing and all the raw edges match. Pin, tack (baste) and stitch along the fold line, taking a 1cm (½in) seam allowance. Turn the binding down and over to the wrong side, to form an edging. Fold in the raw edge of the binding so that it covers the line of machine stitches, and hand stitch in place along the folded edge (see fig 14 page 17).

4. With right sides out and linings facing, place the front and back glasses case shapes together. Pin, tack (baste) and machine stitch round the side and bottom edges taking a 1cm (½in) seam allowance. To finish, bind the side and bottom edges with bias binding.

Bindweed Pincushion

FINISHED DESIGN SIZE
9cm (3½in) square approximately

WHAT YOU WILL NEED
- Cream 14-count Aida, 23cm (9in) square
- Felt for backing, 13cm (5in) square
- Polyester wadding (batting) for filling
- Decorative bias binding, 70cm (¾yd)
- Satin ribbon, enough for four small bows
- Matching sewing thread

DMC STRANDED COTTON (FLOSS)
1 SKEIN
White; light dusty rose 963; very light dusty rose 3716; med dusty rose 962; very light beaver grey 3072; light pale yellow 745; very light avocado green 471; light avocado green 470; avocado green 469

1. Prepare your fabric for work, reading the Techniques section if necessary. Refer to the Stitch Guide pages 11–13 for how to work the stitches, working the design from the centre outwards using the chart on page 110.

2. When stitching the bindweed design use two strands of stranded cotton (floss) for the cross stitch and one strand for the backstitch. Work the backstitch detail in avocado green 469 for the stems, and very light dusty rose 3716 around the flower and its centre.

TO MAKE UP THE PINCUSHION

1. Once the design has been stitched, cut away excess fabric to leave a 13cm (5in) square. Cut a piece of felt to the same size. Place the pieces together, wrong sides facing, and carefully machine stitch 1cm (½in) from the outer edge, leaving a small gap.

2. Fill the pincushion with wadding (batting), slipstitch the gap closed then add decorative bias binding around the edges (see Making Bias Binding page 10 and making up step 3 as for the yellow-horned poppy glasses case). Stitch a small satin ribbon bow at each corner.

Bindweed Heart Garland

FINISHED DESIGN SIZE
3 x 3 x 4cm (1¼ x 1¼ x 1¾in) approximately

WHAT YOU WILL NEED
- Peach 14-count Aida, 20 x 60cm (8 x 24in), enough for three hearts
- Felt for backing, three 20cm (8in) squares
- Polyester wadding (batting) for filling
- Small brass beads
- Satin ribbon, 1m (1⅛yd) enough for three small bows and two hanging loops
- Matching sewing thread

DMC STRANDED COTTON (FLOSS)
1 SKEIN
Use the thread list for the bindweed pincushion

1. Prepare your fabric for work, reading the Techniques section if necessary. Refer to the Stitch Guide on pages 11–13 for the stitches, working the design from the centre outwards.

2. When stitching the design follow the chart on page 110, using two strands of stranded cotton (floss) for the cross stitch and one strand for the backstitch. Work the backstitch detail in avocado green 469 for the stems, and very light dusty rose 3716 around the flower and its centre.

3. Trace the heart template fig 18 on page 126. Cut out this shape and place it centrally over the stitched design, cutting out the shape in Aida. Cut out another heart in the felt backing.

4. Pin the Aida and felt hearts together with right sides facing and machine stitch around the edges, leaving a small gap for turning. Turn the heart right sides out, fill with wadding (batting) then slipstitch the gap closed. Make two more hearts in the same way.

5. Stitch a brass bead between each heart to join them. Stitch a ribbon hanging loop to each end heart (see photograph). Thread brass beads on each ribbon loop and secure with a knot, then stitch ribbon bows to the top of each heart.

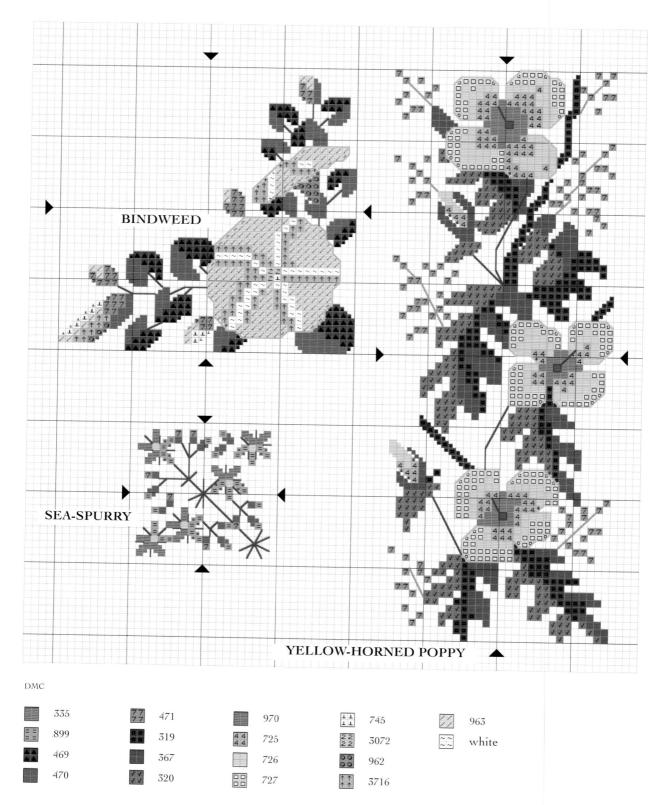

BINDWEED

SEA-SPURRY

YELLOW-HORNED POPPY

DMC

	335		471		970		745		963
	899		319		725		3072		white
	469		367		726		962		
	470		320		727		3716		

Sea Creatures

This wonderful collection of children's accessories decorated with buckets, spades, starfish and sea creatures, is a lovely reminder of seaside holidays. These versatile designs are worked on Aida and 6-count Zweibinca in a variety of colours. Use a mixture of stitches to work up the complete designs, or just pick out elements such as the octopus and sea-horses, or the sailing boats and fishes from the border. Charts have been supplied for each element – starfish, sea-horses, octopus and turtle – so that you can plan your own designs. Try photo-copying the charts, cutting them up and arranging them on a large piece of paper.

DMC STRANDED COTTON (FLOSS)
1 SKEIN

Starfish: Black 310; white; bright orange red 606; light steel grey 318; dark delft blue 798; light brown 434; topaz 725; light tangerine 742; med yellow 743; pale yellow 744; light pale yellow 745. Work the backstitch detail using light tangerine 742 around the starfish body and black 310 to outline each border shape

1 SKEIN

Turtle: Black 310; white; dark delft blue 798; bright orange red 606; light steel grey 318; light brown 434; topaz 725; very light old gold 677; light old gold 676; med old gold 729; dark old gold 680. Work the backstitch detail using light brown 434 around the turtle shell, head and legs, and black 310 to outline each border shape

1 SKEIN

Sea-horse: Black 310; dark delft blue 798; med delft blue 799; very light old gold 677; light old gold 676; med old gold 729; dark old gold 680. Work the backstitch detail using black 310 around each sea-horse body

1 SKEIN

Octopus: Black 310; dark delft blue 798; med delft blue 799; dark orange spice 720; med orange spice 721; light orange spice 722. Work the backstitch detail using dark orange spice 720 around the octopus body

NB: When working the designs on 6 count Zweibinca, you may need more than one skein of some colours

Sea Creatures Rug

FINISHED DESIGN SIZE
Each sea creature design is 21cm (8¼in) square approximately

WHAT YOU WILL NEED
- White 6-count Zweibinca (E3712), 60 x 90cm (24 x 36in)
- Cotton fabric for backing, 60 x 90cm (24 x 36in) wide
- Medium-weight iron-on interfacing, 60 x 90cm (24 x 36in)
- Lightweight polyester wadding (batting), 60 x 90cm (¾yd x 36in)
- Matching sewing threads
- Thick twisted furnishing braid, 2.7m (3yd)

DMC STRANDED COTTON (FLOSS)
Use the thread list (left) for each design element

1. Prepare your fabric for work, reading the Techniques section if necessary. Refer to the Stitch Guide pages 11–13 for how to work the stitches, working the designs from the centre outwards.

111

2. Using the charts work six complete designs, arranged in two rows of three, leaving a 2.5cm (1in) gap between each design as shown in fig 19. Use six strands of stranded cotton (floss) for the cross stitch and three strands for the backstitch over one block of Aida.

Fig 19 Rug layout

TO MAKE UP THE RUG

1. Trim away the excess embroidery fabric to within 6cm (2¼in) of the completed design. Cut a piece of iron-on interfacing to the same size, then iron on to the back of the design to add strength and keep the stitches secure.

2. Cut the cotton backing fabric and polyester wadding (batting) to the same size as the embroidered fabric. Place the backing fabric right side down on a flat surface. Lay the wadding on top, then pin and tack (baste) the two layers together.

3. With right sides facing and the wadding (batting) outwards, pin and tack (baste) the front and back pieces together. Taking a 1.5cm (⅝in) seam allowance, machine stitch all the layers together, leaving a gap along one short edge for turning. Trim away excess wadding to 6mm (¼in), and trim diagonally across each corner to reduce bulk. Turn to the right side, then secure the opening with small slip stitches.

The Sea Creatures Cushions, Stuffed Toys and Baby Bricks, showing the versatility of these designs. The rug is photographed on page 2

4. To make the tasselled braid border, measure the length of the rug edges, then cut lengths of braid to the same measurements, adding 10cm (4in) to each length. Hand stitch the braid along each edge, leaving equal lengths extended at each end. Pinch together the two lengths of braid extending from each corner, then use matching sewing thread to tightly bind them together. Secure the sewing thread with a knot, then fray the braid to make a tassel (fig 20).

Fig 20 Making a tassel

Sea Creatures Cushions

FINISHED DESIGN SIZE
42cm (16½in) square approximately

WHAT YOU WILL NEED FOR ONE CUSHION
- White 6-count Zweibinca, 60cm (24in) square
- Cotton backing fabric, 48cm (19in) square
- Polyester wadding (batting) for filling
- Matching sewing thread
- Thick twisted furnishing braid, 1.3m (1⅜yd)

DMC STRANDED COTTON (FLOSS)
Use the thread list on page 111 for each design element

1. Prepare your fabric for work, reading the Techniques section if necessary. Refer to the Stitch Guide pages 11–13 for how to work the stitches, working the design of your choice from the centre outwards.

2. When stitching the design follow the relevant chart from pages 116–117. Use six strands of stranded cotton (floss) for the cross stitch and three strands for the backstitch, worked over two blocks of threads.

TO MAKE UP THE CUSHION

1. For the cushion front, cut away excess embroidery fabric to within 3cm (1¼in) of the finished design, to allow for a 1.5cm (⅝in) seam allowance.

2. Cut a piece of backing fabric to the same size as the cushion front. With right sides facing, pin, tack (baste) and stitch the cushion front and back together, leaving a 15cm (6in) gap for turning. Turn through to right side, fill with wadding (batting), and secure the opening with slipstitching.

3. To make the tasselled braid border, measure the length of the cushion edges, then follow step 4 on page 113 for the rug.

Sea Creatures Picture

FINISHED DESIGN SIZE
Each design is 12cm (4¾in) square approximately

WHAT YOU WILL NEED
• White 11-count Aida, 28 x 38cm (11 x 15in)

DMC STRANDED COTTON (FLOSS)
Use the thread list on page 111 for each design element

1. Prepare your fabric for work, reading the Techniques section if necessary. Refer to the Stitch Guide pages 11–13 for the stitches, working the design from the centre outwards.

2. Following the charts, work two designs of your choice side by side, placing them 2cm (¾in) apart (see photograph), using three strands of stranded cotton (floss) for the cross stitch and one strand for the backstitch.

3. Refer to Mounting and Framing page 10 for how to complete your picture.

Sea Creatures Stuffed Toys

FINISHED DESIGN SIZES
23cm (9in) square approximately if worked over two threads;
11.5cm (4½in) square approximately if worked over one thread

WHAT YOU WILL NEED
• White 6-count Zweibinca (E3712), 33cm (13in) square for the large design; 20cm (8in) square for the small design
• Felt for backing
• Lightweight polyester wadding (batting)
• Matching sewing thread

DMC STRANDED COTTON (FLOSS)
Use thread list on page 111 for each design element

1. Prepare your fabric for work, reading the Techniques section if necessary. Refer to the Stitch Guide pages 11–13 for how to work the stitches, working the designs from the centre outwards.

2. Follow the relevant charts on page 116–117 to work the designs of your choice. Use six strands of stranded cotton (floss) for the cross stitch and three strands for the backstitch. Work the stitches for the small toys over one block of threads, and over two blocks of threads for the larger toys.

TO MAKE UP THE STUFFED TOYS

1. With a soft pencil, draw a curved line around the completed design to within 1.5cm (⅝in) of the stitches. Trim away excess fabric around this line then cut a piece of felt to the same size as the embroidered fabric.

2. With right sides facing, pin and tack (baste) the front and back pieces together. Taking a 6mm (¼in) seam allowance, machine stitch together, leaving a gap for turning. Make sure all pins are removed. Turn the shape through to right side, fill with wadding (batting), and then secure the opening with slipstitching.

Sea Creatures Baby Bricks

FINISHED DESIGN SIZE
Each complete design is 9.5cm (3¾in) square
approximately

WHAT YOU WILL NEED FOR ONE BRICK
- White, Christmas red and royal blue 14-count Aida
(you will need six 23cm/9in squares for each brick)
- Medium-weight iron-on interfacing 20 x 90cm
(¼yd x 36in) wide
- Polyester wadding (batting)
- Matching sewing thread

DMC STRANDED COTTON (FLOSS)
Use thread list on page 111 for each
design element

1. Prepare your fabric for work, reading the Techniques section if necessary. Refer to the Stitch Guide pages 11–13 for how to work the stitches, working the design from the centre outwards.

2. When stitching the design use two strands of stranded cotton (floss) for the cross stitch and one strand for the backstitch. Using the charts overleaf work up six squares choosing a mixture of designs for each brick.

TO MAKE UP A BRICK

1. Trim away excess Aida fabric from around the design, to leave a 15cm (6in) square. Cut a piece of iron-on interfacing to the same size, then carefully iron the interfacing on to the back of the design to give added strength to the fabric and help keep the embroidered stitches secure.

2. Use one square as a base, then, with right sides facing, pin, and tack (baste) an embroidered square onto each of the four edges of the base square. Stitch along the seams taking a 1cm (½in) seam allowance. Press the seams open. Fold each square upwards, so that the sides meet, with right sides facing then stitch the matching sides together.

3. To finish the cube, pin, tack (baste) and stitch the remaining square in place. Stitch along three edges, leaving one edge open. Make sure all pins are removed then turn right side out. Fill with wadding (batting), then slipstitch the gap to close.

Below: The Sea Creatures Picture featuring the starfish and turtle from the Sea Creatures designs

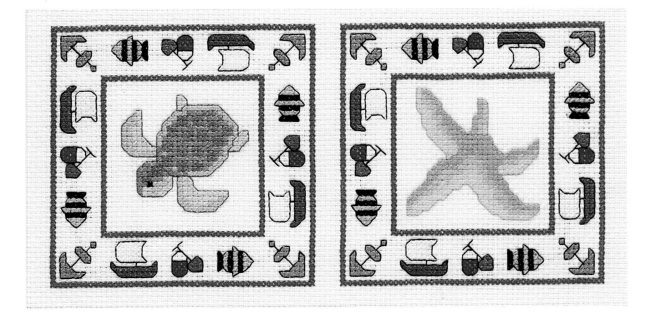

STARFISH
DMC

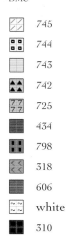

▨	745
▣	744
	743
▲▲	742
7 7	725
▦	434
▦	798
◺	318
▦	606
∼∼	white
▦	310

TURTLE
DMC

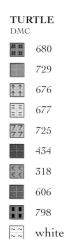

▦	680
	729
↑↑	676
═ ═	677
7 7	725
▦	434
◺	318
▦	606
▣	798
∼∼	white
▦	310

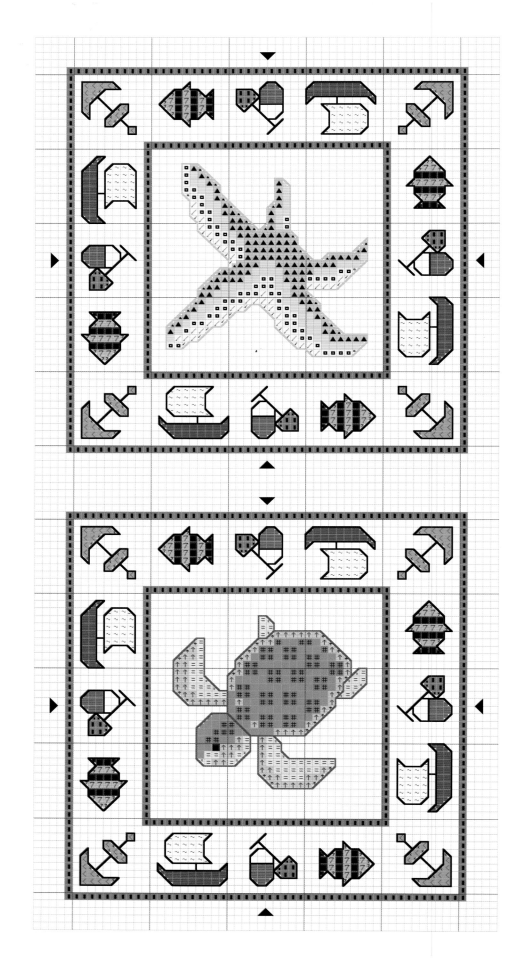

SEAHORSE
DMC

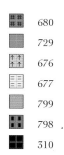

⊞⊞	680
	729
↑↑	676
☰☰	677
	799
▦	798
■	310

OCTOPUS
DMC

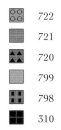

◯◯	722
	721
▲▲	720
	799
▦	798
■	310

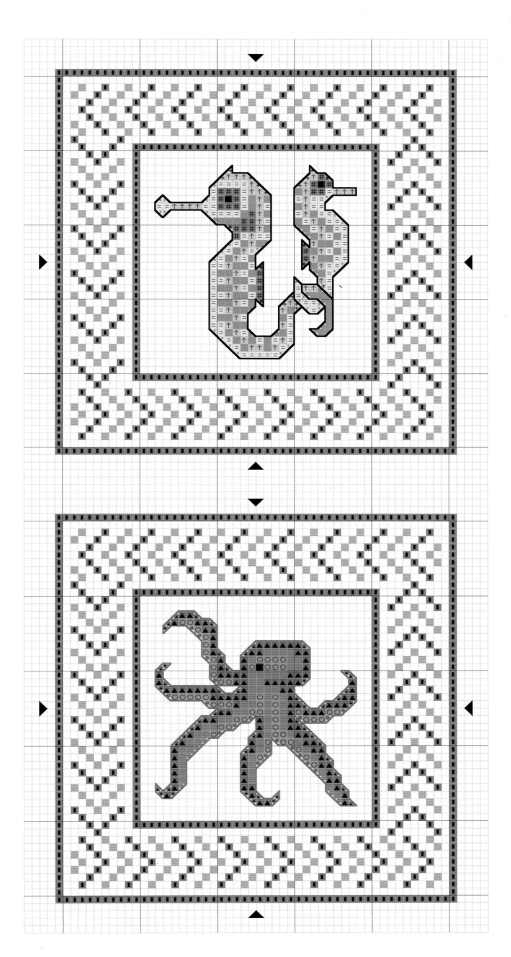

Polar Bears Picture

This snowy scene shows a mother polar bear and her cubs on the arctic ice flows,
set against a dark blue sky. Cubs raised in this harsh environment stay close to their mother.
When they swim in the freezing arctic waters, they cling to her tail for security. Shades
of white, pale yellow and light grey are used to stitch the bears' white coats, camouflaged
against the blue-white snow and pack-ice. The background snow is worked with a
mixture of metallic threads and stranded cotton (floss), to make it glisten. A mixture of
cross stitch, three-quarter cross stitch, backstitch and French knots are used to
work this design on a dark blue 14-count Aida.

POLAR BEAR

These are the most northerly species of bear found in the Arctic circle, where they spend most of their time on the pack-ice or ice-flows feeding on seals. Polar bears have broad, flat feet with furred soles to act as snow-shoes, and white coats as camouflage against snow and ice. They used to be hunted in large numbers, and still are today by the Inuit who eat them and use their skins for clothing and bedding. Inuit mythology believed that these creatures were sacred and that their spirits were shamans or spiritual guides. When bears walk on their hind legs, they look rather like humans, and so it was believed that bear and human spirits were interchangeable.

FINISHED DESIGN SIZE
20 x 28cm (7⅞in x 11in) approximately

WHAT YOU WILL NEED
• Cadet blue 14-count Aida, 33 x 43cm (13 x 17in)

DMC STRANDED COTTON (FLOSS)
1 SKEIN
Black 310; very light old gold 677; light old gold 676; med beige grey 644; dark beige grey 642; very dark pewter grey 640; dark beige grey 3790; very light antique blue 3753; very light antique blue 3752; light antique blue 932; med antique blue 931; very dark antique blue 3750; very light grey green 928; light grey green 927; light grey green 926; dark grey green 3768; very dark grey green 924; dark pewter grey 413; pewter grey 317
2 SKEINS
White; off-white 746

DMC METALLIC STRANDED COTTON (FLOSS)
1 SKEIN
Silver 1000

1. Prepare your fabric for work, reading the Techniques section if necessary. Refer to the Stitch Guide pages 11–13 for how to work the stitches, working from the centre outwards.
2. When stitching the design use two strands of stranded cotton (floss) for the cross stitch and one strand for the backstitch and French knots. For the background area work the areas of white cross stitch by using one strand of white and one strand of silver mixed together.
3. Work the backstitch detail in black 310 around the eyes, mouths and noses, and dark beige grey 3790 around the ears. Use white to work a small French knot for the eye highlights.
4. Refer to Mounting and Framing page 10 for how to complete your picture.

DMC

644	3753	927	413
676	3790	928	924
677	640	3750	white
746	642	931	310
932	3768	1000 (silver)	
3752	926	317	

Emperor Penguins Picture

*Except for their size, it would be difficult to identify a penguin from its body alone
as most of their distinguishing features appear on their head and neck. The adults in this
group of Emperor penguins are easily recognised by the yellow colouring on their cheeks, neck
and upper chest, whilst the babies are just a mass of fluffy grey feathers. This design is worked
in cross stitch, three-quarter cross stitch, backstitch and French knots, on a white 14-count
Aida, which makes the black and yellow colouring really stand out.*

FINISHED DESIGN SIZE
20 x 33cm (7¾ x 13in) approximately

WHAT YOU WILL NEED
• White 14-count Aida, 38 x 48cm (15 x 19in)

DMC STRANDED COTTON (FLOSS)
1 SKEIN
Very dark pewter grey 3799; dark pewter grey 413;
pewter grey 317; dark steel grey 414; light steel grey
318; pearl grey 415; very light pearl grey 762; light pale
yellow 745; pale yellow 744; med yellow 743; light tangerine 742; med tangerine 741; tangerine 740; dark red
copper 918; med copper 920; very dark mahogany 300;
light old gold 676; med old gold 729; dark old gold 680;
very light antique violet 3743; light antique violet 3042;
med antique violet 3041; very light antique blue 3753;
very light antique blue 3752; light antique blue 932
2 SKEINS
Black 310; very pale yellow 3823
3 SKEINS
White

1. Prepare your fabric for work, reading the
Techniques section if necessary. Refer to the
Stitch Guide pages 11–13 for the stitches,
working the design from the centre outwards.

2. When stitching the design use two strands of
stranded cotton (floss) for the cross stitch and
French knots, and one strand for the backstitch.
Work the backstitch detail in black 310 to
outline the eyes, and use white to work a small
French knot for the eye highlights.

3. Refer to Mounting and Framing on page 10
for advice on how to complete your Emperor
Penguins Picture.

PENGUINS
Penguins have been around for millions of
years and can be found all over the southern
hemisphere and even in some tropical climates.
When King penguins were first described in
1775, it was thought that the adults and fluffy
babies where two different species. Early
explorers thought that penguins were fish
because they couldn't fly, used their wings to
swim, and had short legs which made walking
awkward. In the 1800s, penguins were killed in
huge numbers for their oil.

DMC

	932		3041		680		300		740
	3752		3042		729		920		741
	3753		3743		676		918		742

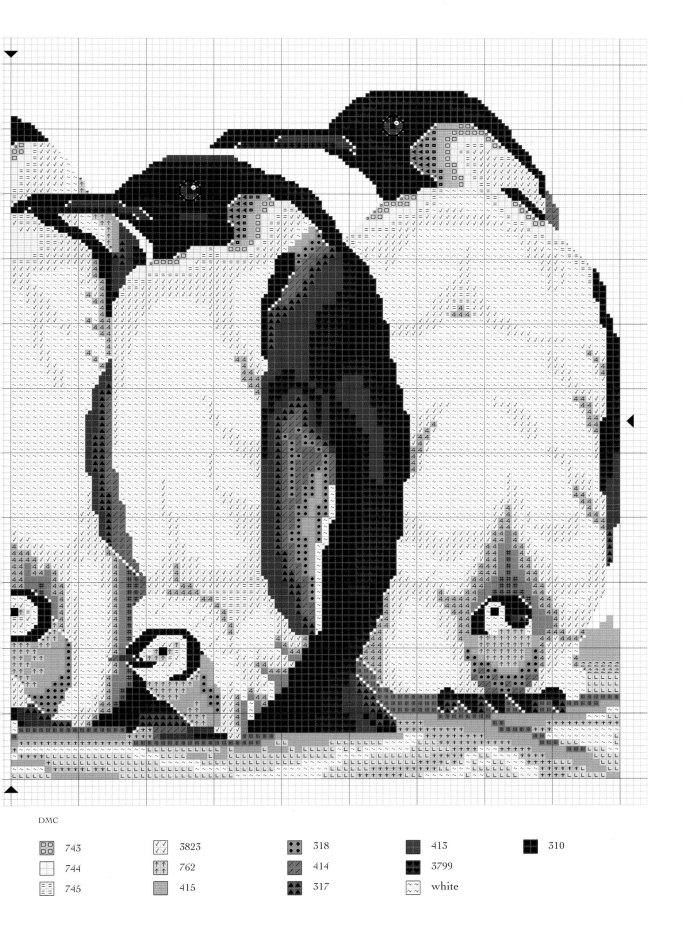

DMC

▦ 743	✓ 3823	● 318	■ 413	■ 310
▦ 744	↑ 762	▨ 414	▨ 3799	
▤ 745	▨ 415	▲ 317	≈ white	

Acknowledgements

We would both like to give a special thank you to our long-suffering husbands, Ian and Tim, for all their support whilst Jayne and I worked frantically on this book. Thank you to our families for being so patient and putting up with us. Thank you also to the following people for their contributions and help with getting this book published. Vivienne Wells, as always. Doreen Montgomery for her invaluable advice and support. Cheryl Brown and Kay Ball at David & Charles for their help and advice with the production of the book. A big thank you to Di Lewis for the wonderful photography, which really makes the book sparkle, and to David Lynch for the photo on the back cover flap. Thank you also to Cara Ackerman, Sarah Gray, Gleyns Black-Roberts and Susan Haigh, and to John Parkes of Outpost Trading for his excellent picture framing skills.

Fig 18 Heart template

Stockists

If you should require any further information about products, catalogues, price lists or local stockists from any of the suppliers mentioned, contact them direct by post or phone. Please remember to always include a stamped addressed envelope. If contacting them by phone, they will be able to tell you if there is any charge for the catalogue or price lists.

DMC Creative World, Pullman Road, Wigston, Leicester LE18 2DY. Tel: (0116) 281 1040. For all threads and embroidery fabrics used throughout the book, and for the name and address of your nearest DMC and Zweigart stockist.

DMC threads are supplied in the USA by The DMC Corporation, Port Kearny, Building 10, South Kearny, NJ 07032.
Zweigart fabric is supplied in the USA by Joan Toggitt Ltd, 2 River View Drive, Somerset, NJ 08873.

Framecraft Miniatures Ltd, 372–376 Summer Lane, Hockley, Birmingham B19 3QA. Tel: (0121) 212 0551. Suppliers of the wooden and brass trays, dressing-table set, brass powder puff, mantle clock, bell pull hanging rods, desk accessories, key ring and coasters. They also supply Mill Hill Beads in the UK.

Framecraft products are also supplied worldwide by:
Anne Brinkley Designs Inc, 761 Palmer Avenue, Holmdel, NJ 97733, USA;
Gay Bowles Sales Inc, PO Box 1060, Janesville, WI 53547, USA;
Ireland Needlecraft Pty Ltd, 4, 2–4 Keppel Drive, Hallam, Vic 3803, Australia.

MacGregor Designs, PO Box 129, Burton upon Trent, DE14 3XH. Tel: (01283) 702117 for mail order catalogue of specialist woodwork accessories. Suppliers of the square footstool (Dolphin design).

Market Square (Warminster) Ltd, Wing Farm, Longbridge Deverill, Warminster, Wilts, BA12 7DD. Tel: (01985) 841042. Suppliers of the fire-screen for the Clipper Ship design.

Vilene products were used on projects throughout the book. A selection of iron-on interfacings are available in major deparment stores and all good haberdashery shops (notions departments).

Some of the designs included in this book are available in kit form by mail. For further details contact: The Janlynn Corporation, 34 Front Street, PO Box 51848, Indian Orchard, MA 01151-5848, USA. At the time of publication, 'Dolphins', 'Brown Bears' and 'Flamingos' were available in kit form.

Index